THE RAILWAY CHILDREN

Book and Lyrics by Julian Woolford   **Music by Richard John**

From the novel by E. Nesbit

Vocal Selections

Samuel French – London
New York-Toronto-Hollywood

The Railway Children was first produced at Sevenoaks Playhouse, on the 3rd December 2005, with the following cast:

Perks	Paul Henry
Father	Charles Shirvell
Mother	Susannah Fellows
Peter	Chris Crompton
Carol Singers	Maria Holley, Neil Ditt and Brendan Cull
Cook	Karen Clegg
Ruth	Claire Taylor
Roberta (Bobbie)	Emily Bull
Phyllis	Lucy Brushett*
Mr Barrie	Brendan Cull
Dr Forrest	Neil Ditt
Lord Fleet	Charles Shirvell
Mrs Ransome	Claire Taylor
Gert	Maria Holley
Mrs Perks	Karen Clegg
Old Gentleman	Nicholas Smith
Rushing Man	Brendan Cull
Szczepansky	Charles Shirvell
Engine Driver	Neil Ditt
Jim	Brendan Cull
Londoners	Claire Taylor, Maria Holley and Karen Clegg
Vendor	Charles Shirvell
Customer	Neil Ditt

Children's Chorus
Megan Barker, Georgia Brown, Hollie Evans, Rebecca Hairs, Rosie Jenner, Emma Sweet, Karl Warner, James Webster, Charlotte Wilson, Jade Wood, Stephanie Barrett, Oliver Christopher, Sophie Cook, Olivia Davey, Laura Hayward, Leanne Kyte, Annabelle Lake, Glyn Pritchard, Kiri Rayner, Paige Stapleton

*The role of Phyllis was shared with Rachel Bartholomeusz

Director	Julian Woolford
Musical Supervisor	Richard John
Choreographer	Chris Hocking
Set Designer	Charles Camm
Lighting Designer	Emma Chapman
Sound Designer	Dominic Bilkey
Costume Supervisor	Rodney Worth
Musical Director	Laurence Mark Wythe
Vocal & Dance Arrangements	Richard John
Russian Translation	Simon Hollands
Photography	Robert Workman

The original cast recording is available on TER and JAY records.
Vocal score and orchestral parts are available on hire from Samuel French Ltd.

THE RAILWAY CHILDREN

Book and Lyrics by Julian Woolford **Music by Richard John**

From the novel by E. Nesbit

Vocal Selections

Contents

Synopsis .... p 4

Together .... p 6

All On Time .... p 13

Posh Talk .... p 32

The Railway Children .... p 43

'Til The Day .... p 51

A Once In A Lifetime Day .... p 64

Busy Dreaming .... p 85

Nothing To Fear .... p 93

One Voice .... p 97

Nearly Autumn .... p 116

Arrangements edited by Richard John

In 1905, one hundred years prior to the premiere of this musical, Edith Nesbit first published The Railway Children in serial form in The London Magazine. In 1906, the episodes were gathered together and it was published as a novel. This songbook includes the major songs from the musical (listed in bold typeface below). Most dance breaks have been reduced or removed, and new arrangements have been made of several songs to make them appropriate for concert performance.

Julian Woolford and Richard John, London 2007

SYNOPSIS

Mr Perks, the Stationmaster, remembers how the story began, in a family home in London one Christmas *(Prologue: Christmas is Here!)*. The family, Father, Mother, daughters Roberta (Bobbie) and Phyllis and son Peter (who has opened his gift, a toy railway) are the model of a happy family. Ruth, the maid, tells Father that two gentlemen have arrived to see him. Father goes to meet them and Ruth returns to tell the children that Christmas is cancelled (*You Can Never Return*).

Mother and the children are then discovered at Charing Cross Station, ready to depart to a new life in the country. Mother will not tell them where Father has gone, but not to worry – they will still be **Together**. At the end of the number they arrive at their new home. It is cold, damp, dark and there are no servants (*Together Reprise*).

Next morning, the children find a railway line nearby and watch as trains run by. They think it looks like a great green dragon and, as they wave, they ask it to take their love to Father, wherever he is. In the last carriage of the train they see an Old Gentleman, waving back at them.

They arrive at the station, and meet Mr Perks who tells them of the wonder of the railway and introduces them to the other villagers **(All On Time)**. That evening, Mother is taken ill and Doctor Forrest tells Bobbie that she must have certain foods to make her better. Mother tells Bobbie that they cannot afford this, but Bobbie, Peter and Phyllis come up with a plan to ask the Old Gentleman in the train for help (*You Might Make A Friend*)..

Perks brings a package from the Old Gentleman, containing all the food they need – and more. Mother is angry that they have asked a stranger for help and sends them to the station with a thank you letter for the Old Gentleman

At the station they meet some of the local children, and after initial hostilities, make friends **(Posh Talk)**. A train arrives and a strange foreigner alights, clearly lost. Bobbie sends Phyllis to get Mother, who is able to converse with the man in French. She tells the villagers that Mr Szczepansky is a Russian dissident writer who has escaped from a gulag and has come to England to find his wife and child, who he believes are there. She takes the Russian man to her cottage where he can recover from his illness (*Russian Lullaby*).

The children want to help Mr Szczepansky become reunited with his family, and write to the Old Gentleman asking for his help **(The Railway Children)**.

Mother sends the children on a picnic, but Bobbie returns to find Mother crying. The thought of a picnic has made Mother remember the wonderful times they all had with Father, and after Bobbie has left, she longs for her husband (**'Til The Day**).

Picnicking on the hillside the children witness a landslide, which blocks the line. Realizing that the train is due and will crash if they do not intervene, the children create red flags from the girls' red bloomers and wave them at the train as it leaves the tunnel. The train stops, just in time.

Act Two opens with the entire village celebrating the children's bravery at an award ceremony where the children are given commemorative watches *(**A Once-In-A-Lifetime Day**)*. As the crowd disperses, Mother thanks the Old Gentleman (who is a Director of the Railway) for his help when she was ill. He asks to see Mr Szczepansky, announcing that he has found the Russian's family, they are living in Oxford and they can be reunited that afternoon.

As the family go to help the Russian pack, Bobbie asks the Old Gentleman how he is always able to help. He explains his philosophy *(**Busy Dreaming**)*.

Weeks later, the children watch a group of grammar schoolboys on a cross country race *(Paperchase Ballet)*. They notice that one of the boys entered the railway tunnel, but hasn't come out the other side. They enter the tunnel and find him, injured by the trackside. Bobbie sends Peter and Phyllis back to get help *(**Nothing To Fear**)*, and, once home, Dr Forrest tells Bobbie that Mother has gone to meet a relative of the boy, Jim. Peter and Phyllis arrive with some medicine for Jim, wrapped in newspaper. Bobbie notices a news story and, starting to cry, tells her siblings to leave her alone.

Mother returns with Jim's grandfather: none other than their dear Old Gentleman. Sending the Old Gentleman upstairs with Peter and Phyllis, Mother asks Bobbie why she is crying. Bobbie shows Mother the newspaper, which carries a story of Father's imprisonment on spying charges. Mother is finally able to tell Bobbie the whole story of how Father has been wrongfully imprisoned and Bobbie asks the Old Gentleman for help.

The Old Gentleman, sure of Father's innocence, teaches Bobbie a poem penned by her friend Szczepansky. Still keeping Father's fate from Peter and Phyllis, Mother and Bobbie return to London to campaign for Father's release *(**One Voice**)*.

Jim's broken leg now healed, he leaves the Three Chimneys cottage to return to school, but not before promising Bobbie he will write and gently kissing her. The children go to see the railway again, but, this time, notice the Old Gentleman, and all the other passengers waving to them *(Who Knows What You'll Find)*. Bobbie, emotional after Jim's affection, sends Peter and Phyllis home, and sets out on a walk alone *(**Nearly Autumn**)*.

She meets Mrs Ransome, the postmistress, who tells her of a telegram that has arrived for Mother. She tells Bobbie to rush to the station. At the station, a crowd has gathered, and everyone is in a state of high excitement. A train arrives and, as the smoke clears, Bobbie sees a figure. It is her Father. The family, having received the telegram, arrive at the station to be reunited at last *(Finale)*.

Together

The Railway Children

Lyrics by Julian Woolford　　　　　　　　　　　　　　　　　　　Music by Richard John

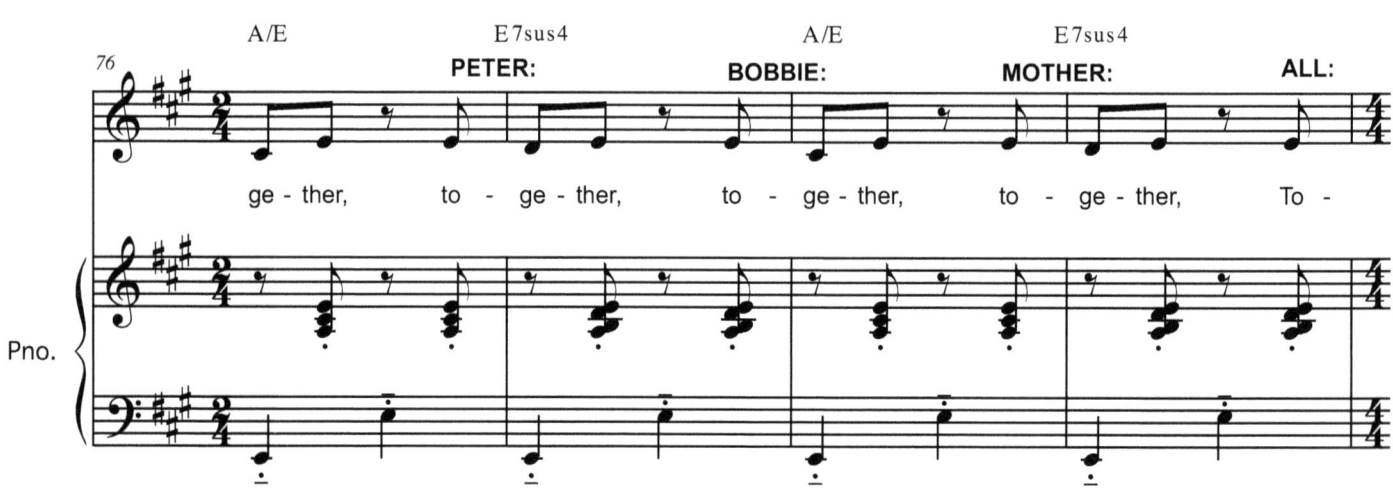

All On Time

The Railway Children

Lyrics by Julian Woolford
Music by Richard John

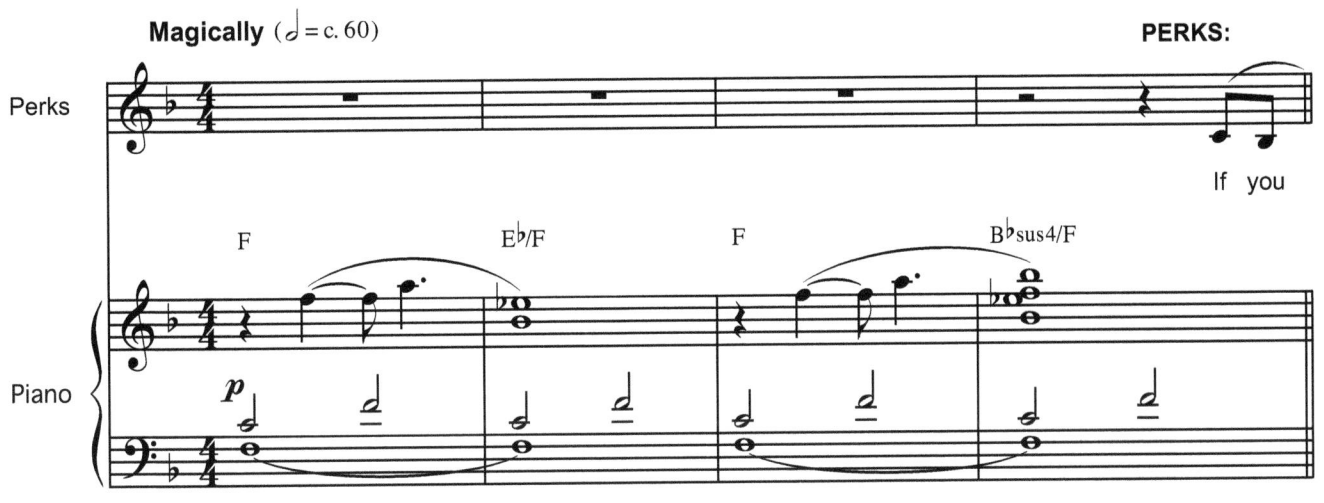

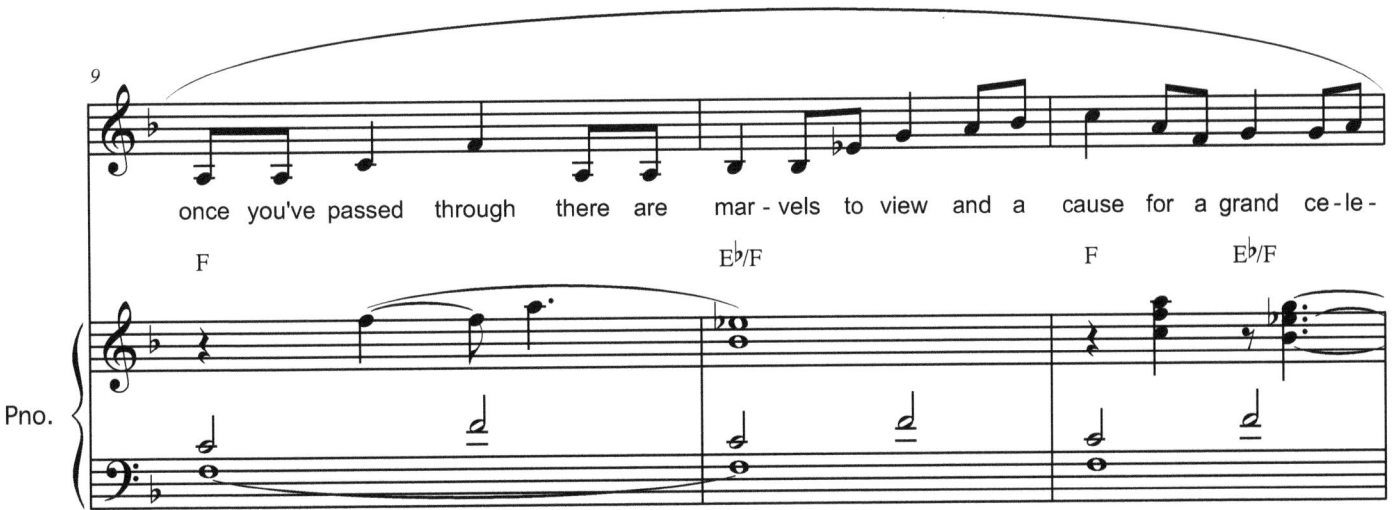

Copyright © Woolford & John 2007
International Copyright Secured. All Rights Reserved.

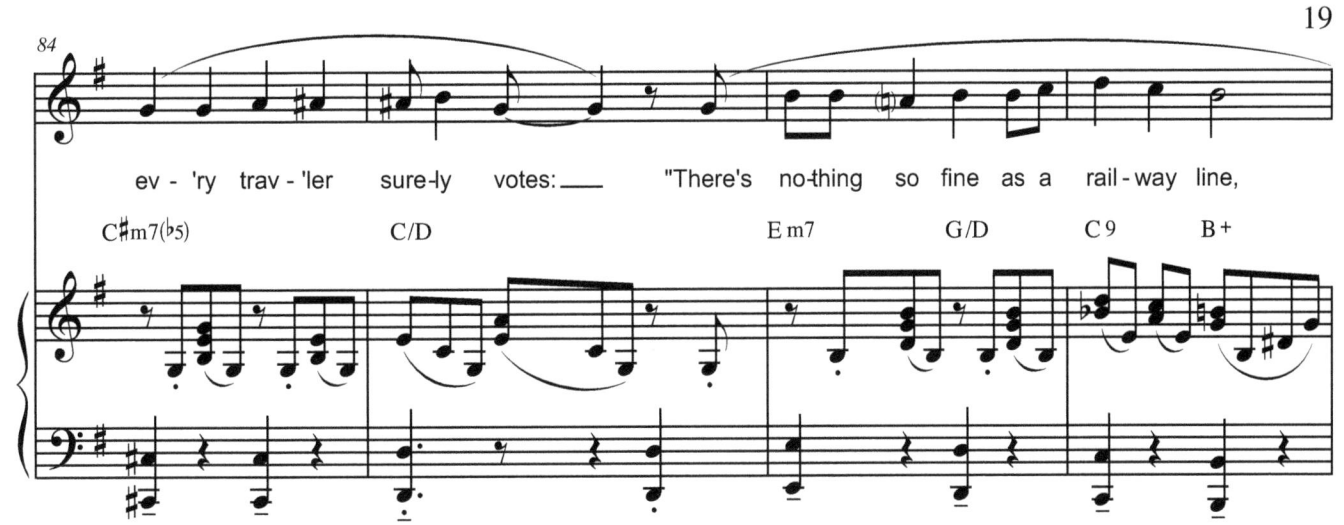
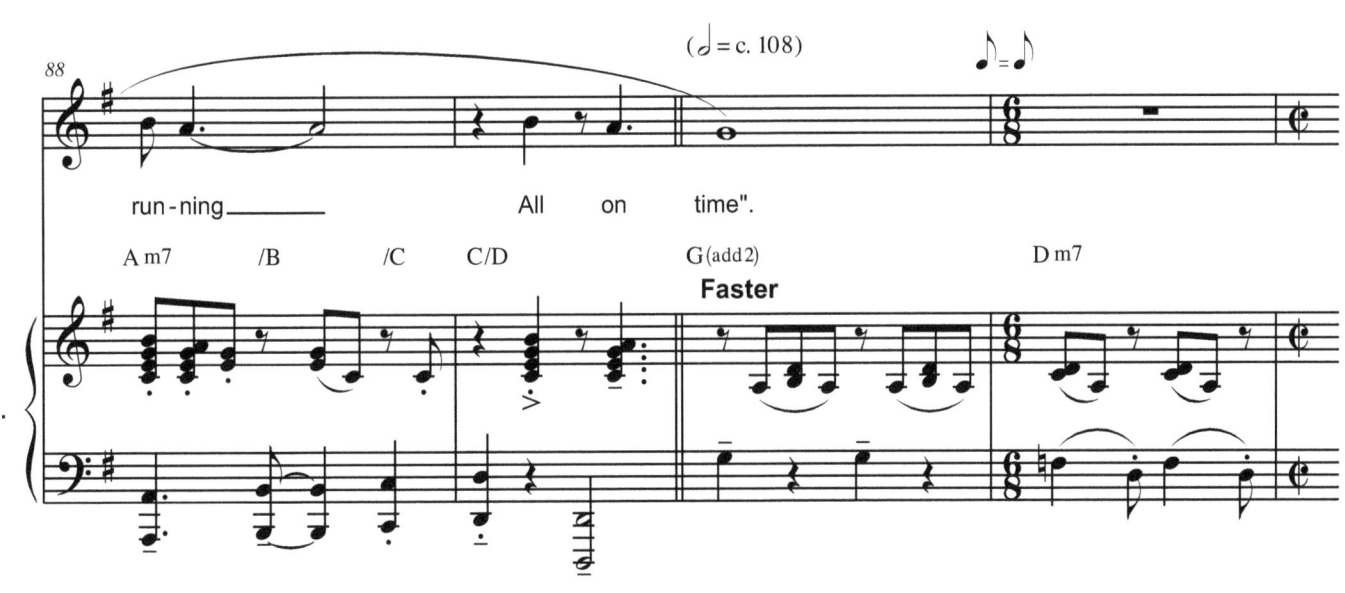

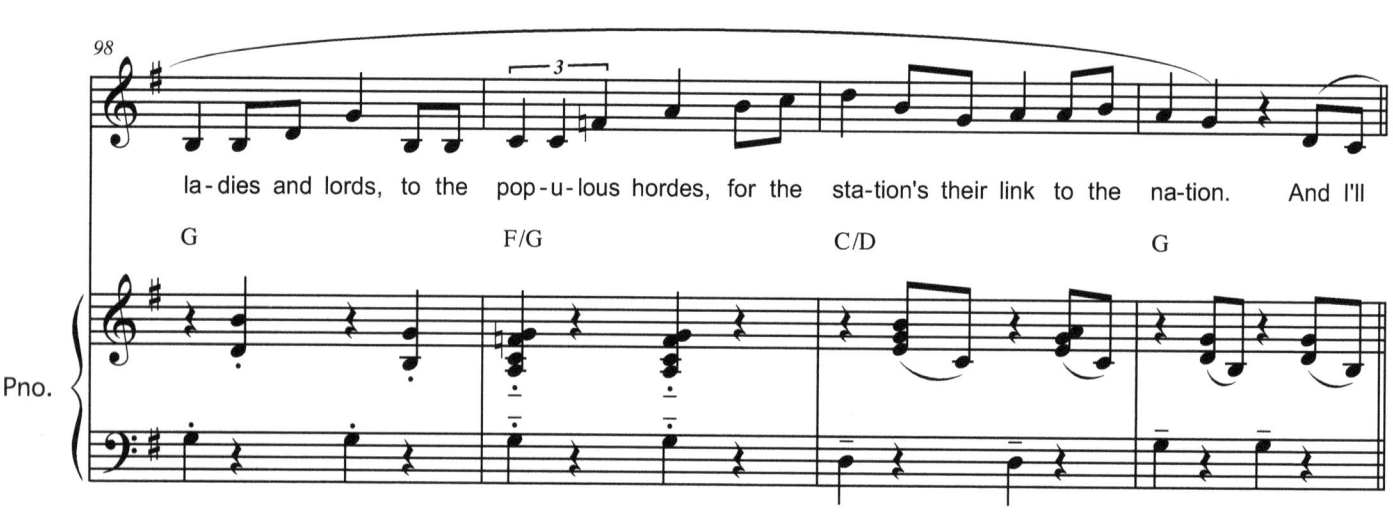

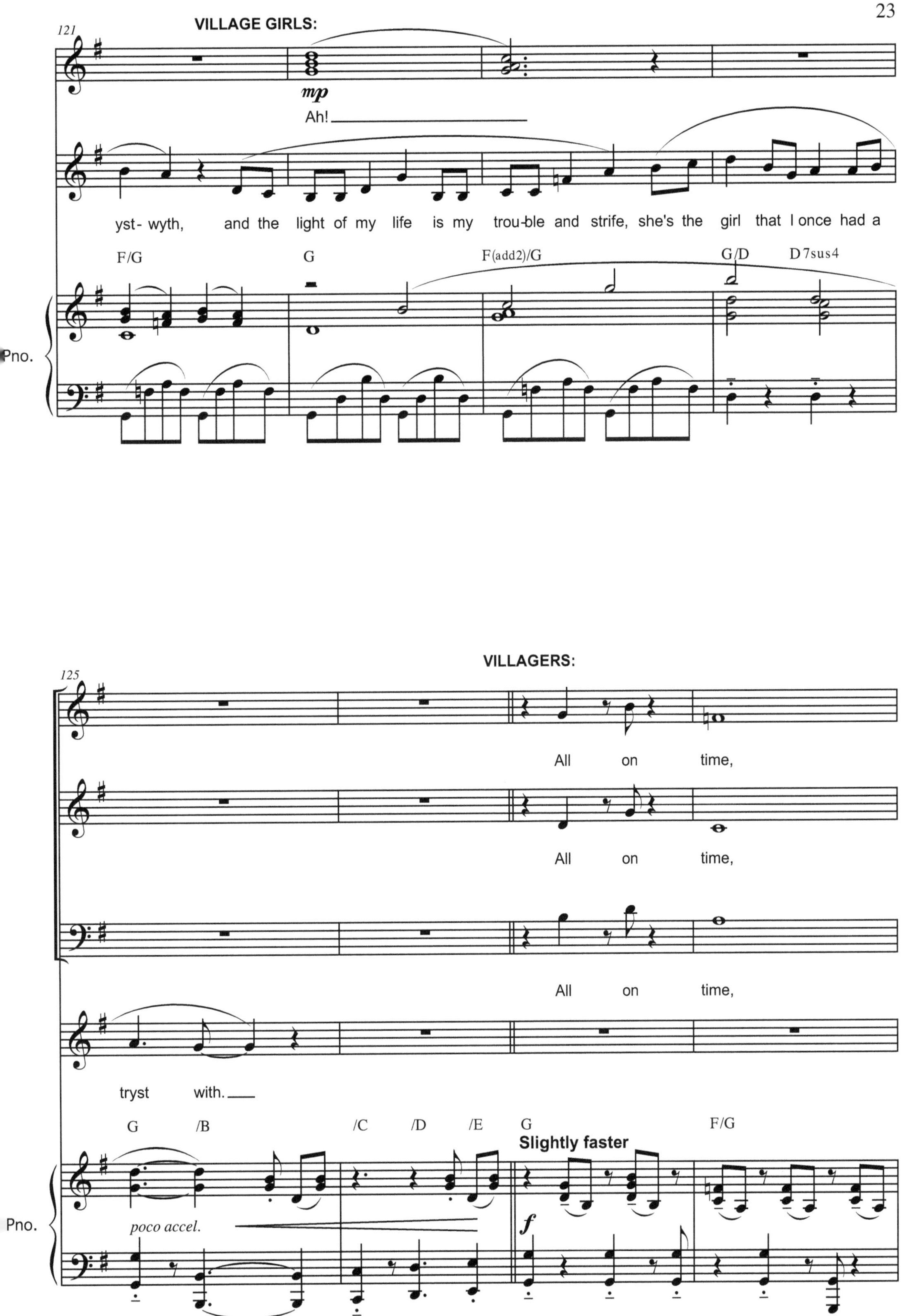
121
VILLAGE GIRLS:
mp
Ah!
yst- wyth, and the light of my life is my trou-ble and strife, she's the girl that I once had a
F/G
G
F(add2)/G
G/D
D7sus4
Pno.
125
VILLAGERS:
All on time,
All on time,
All on time,
tryst with.
G
/B
/C
/D
/E
G
F/G
Slightly faster
poco accel.
f
Pno.

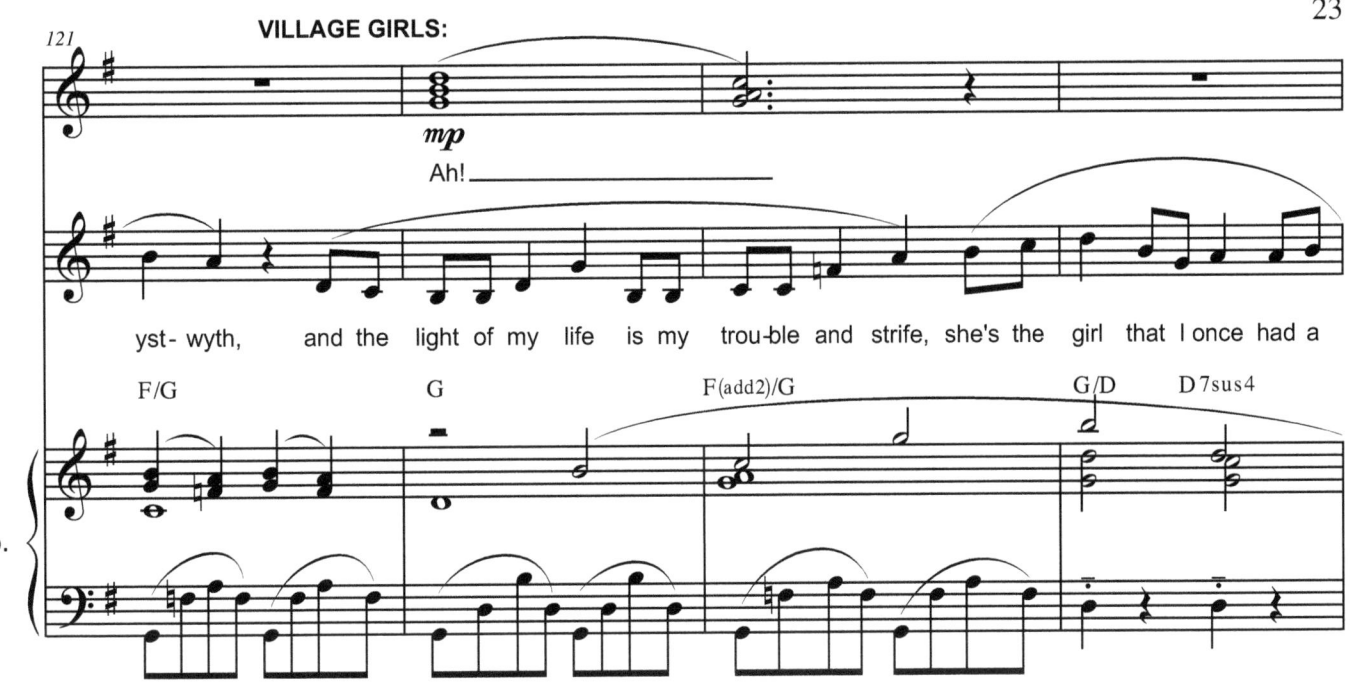

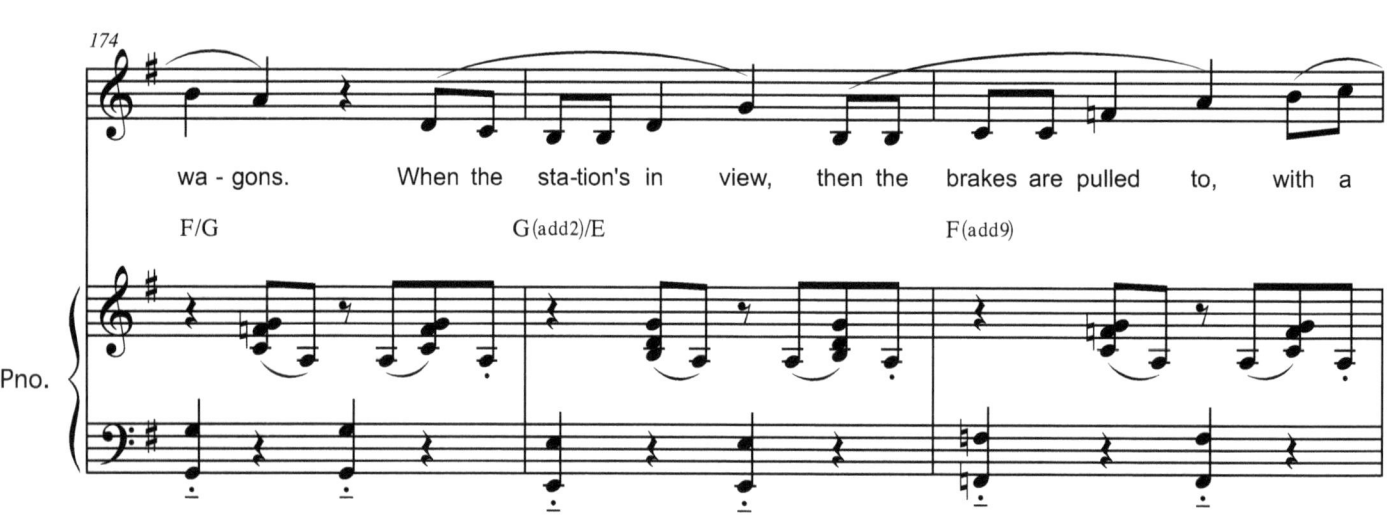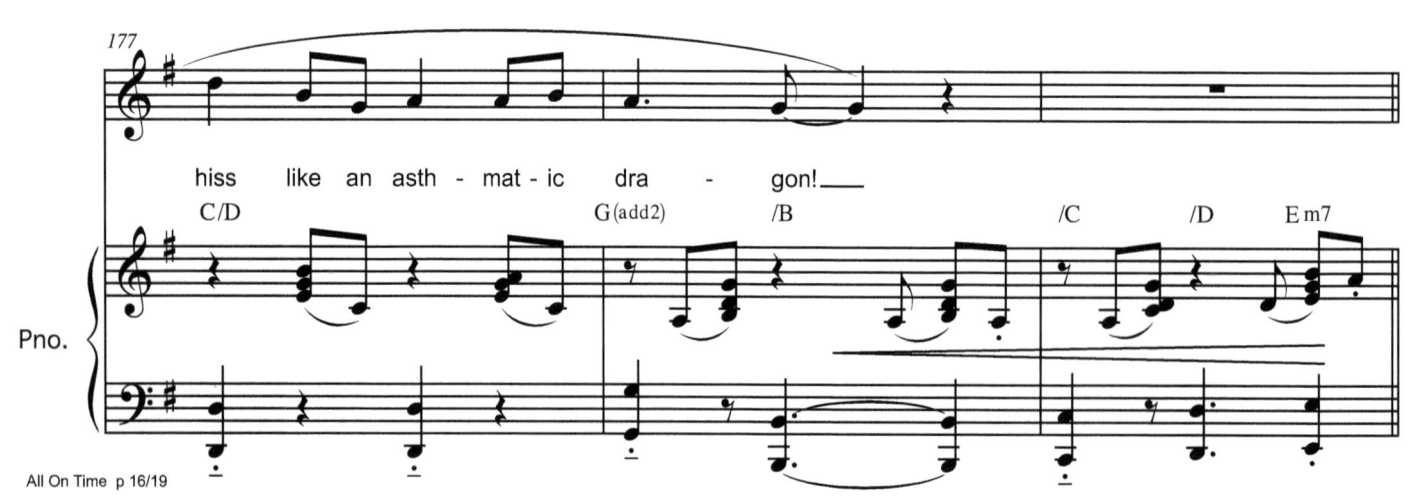

Posh Talk

Lyrics by Julian Woolford

The Railway Children

Music by Richard John

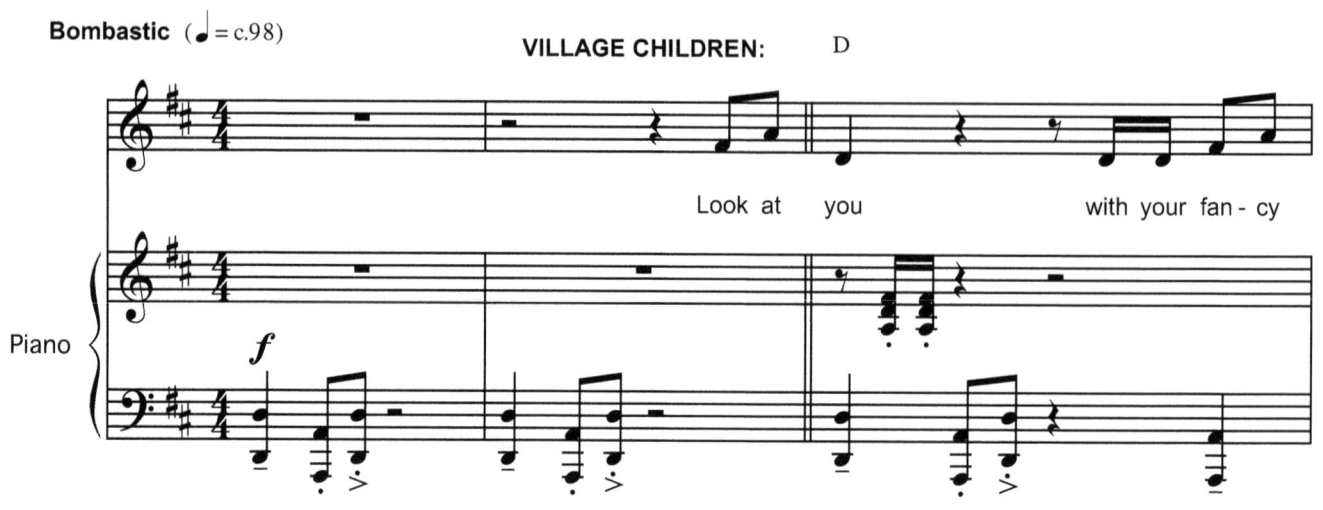

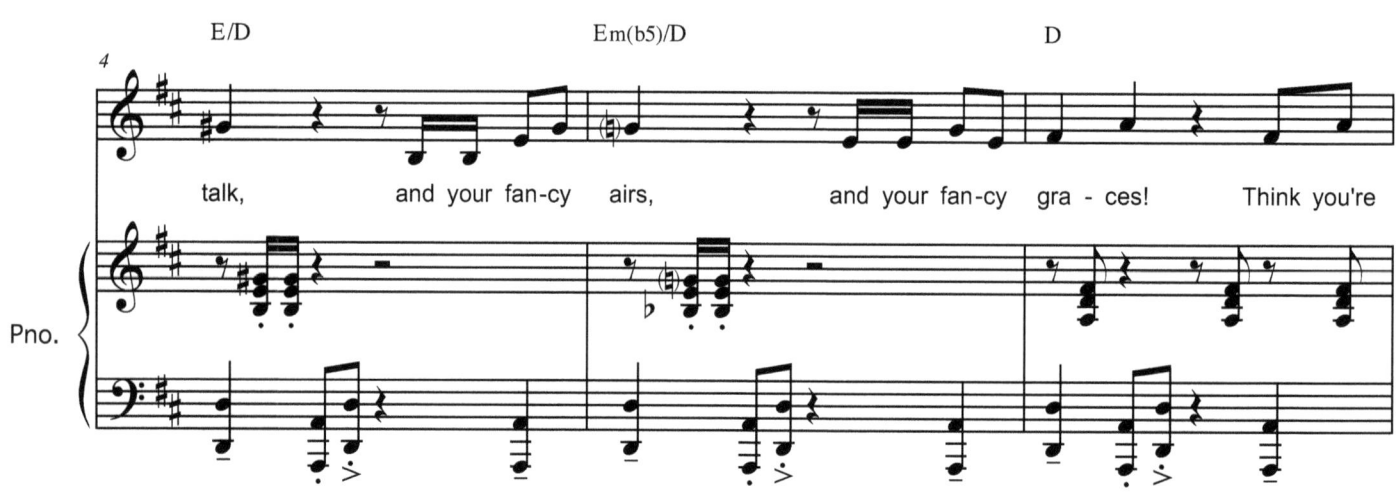

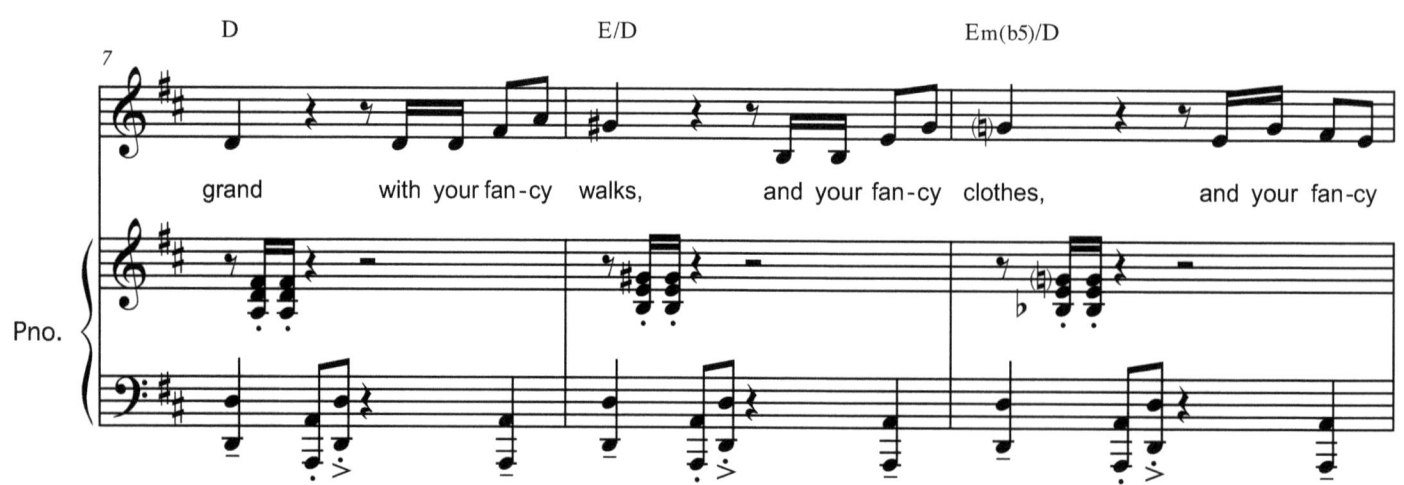

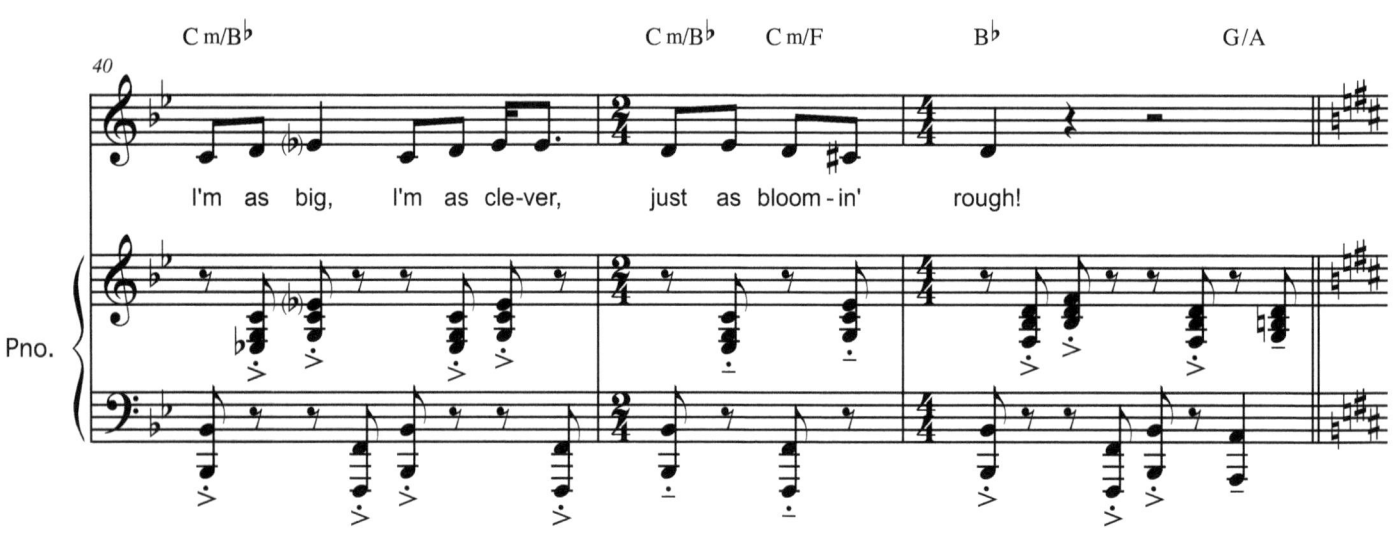
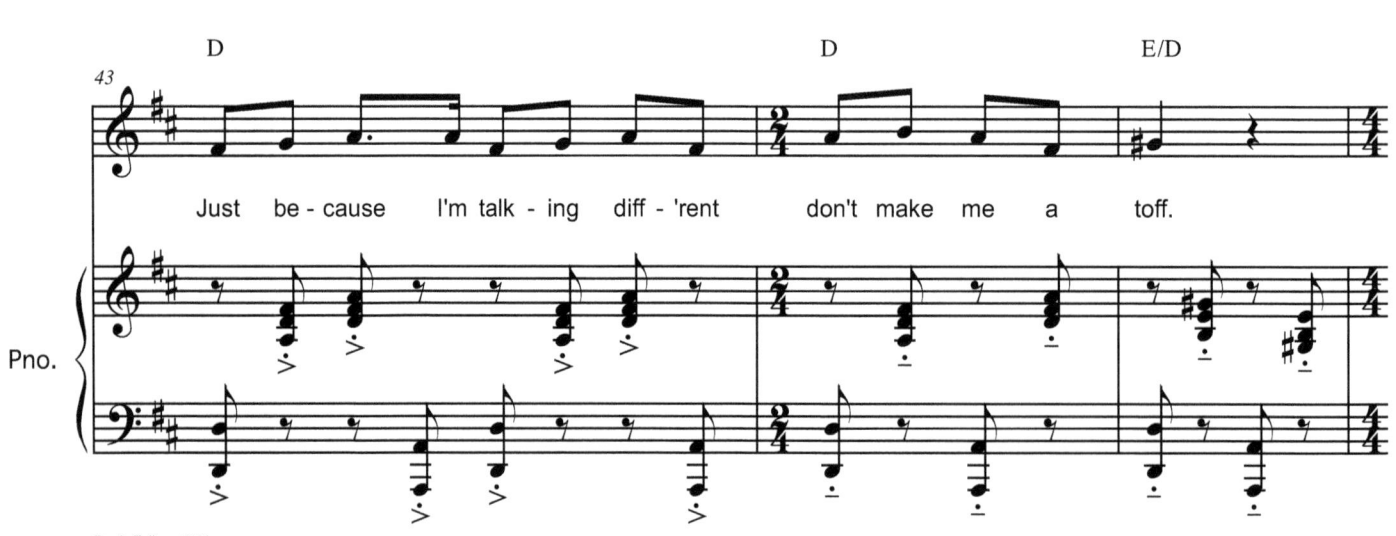

Posh Talk p 5/11

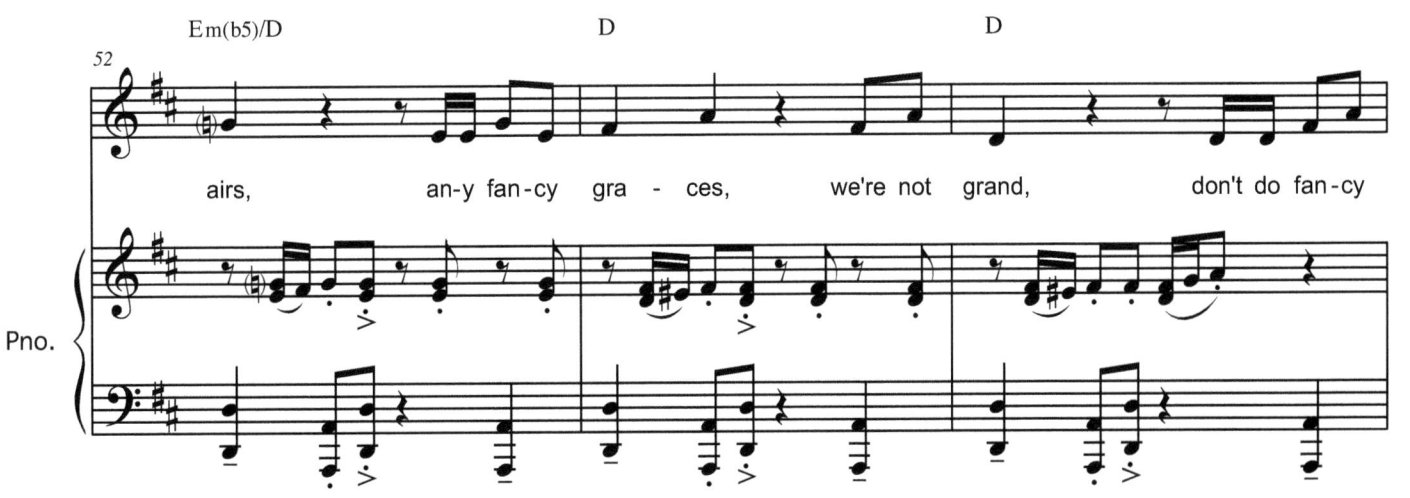

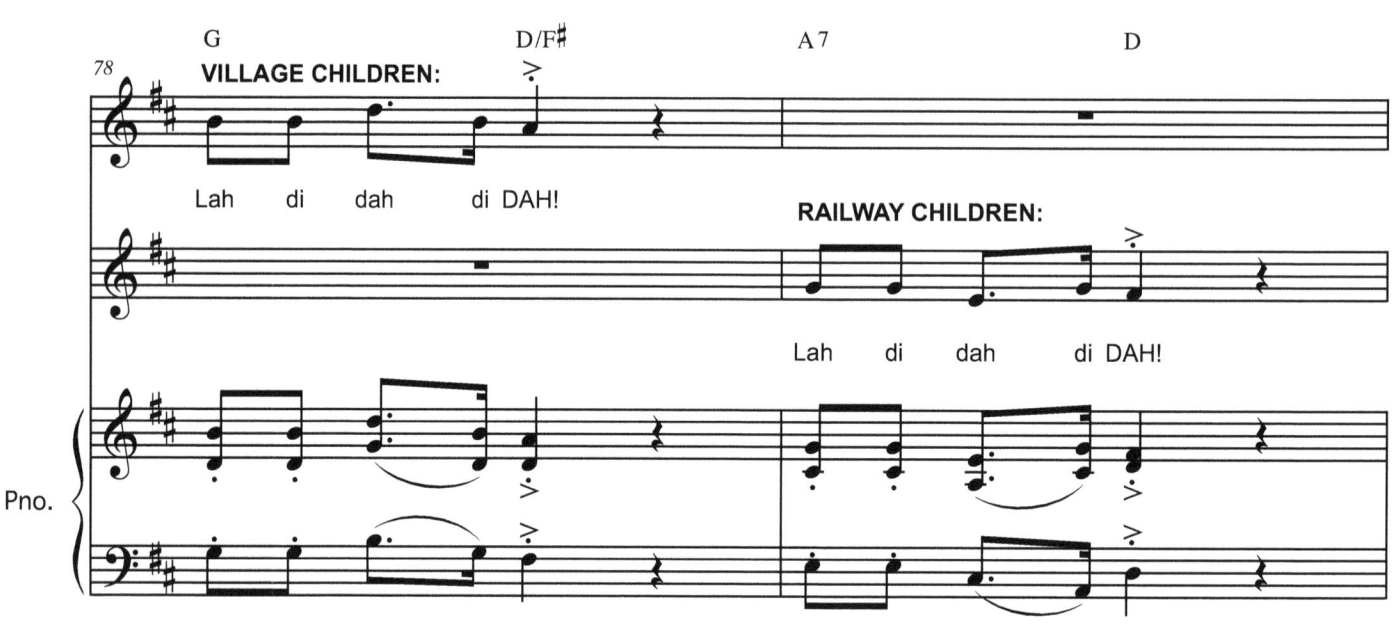
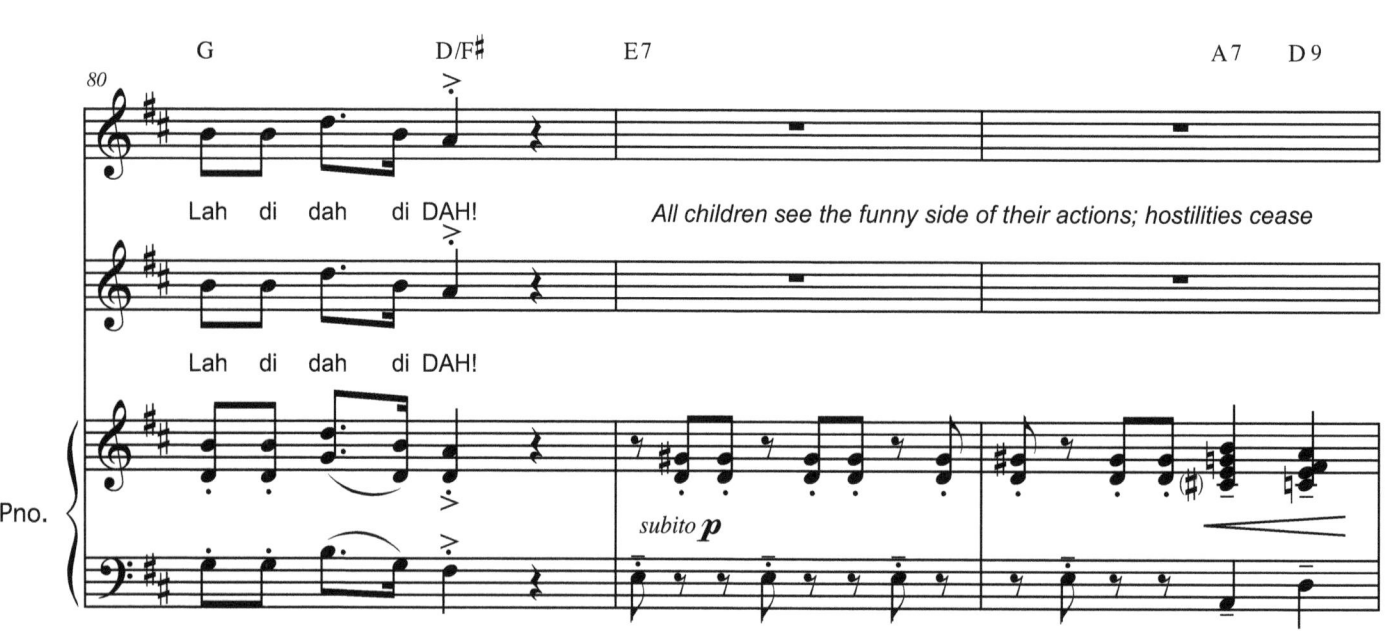

All children see the funny side of their actions; hostilities cease

The Railway Children

Lyrics by Julian Woolford

The Railway Children

Music by Richard John

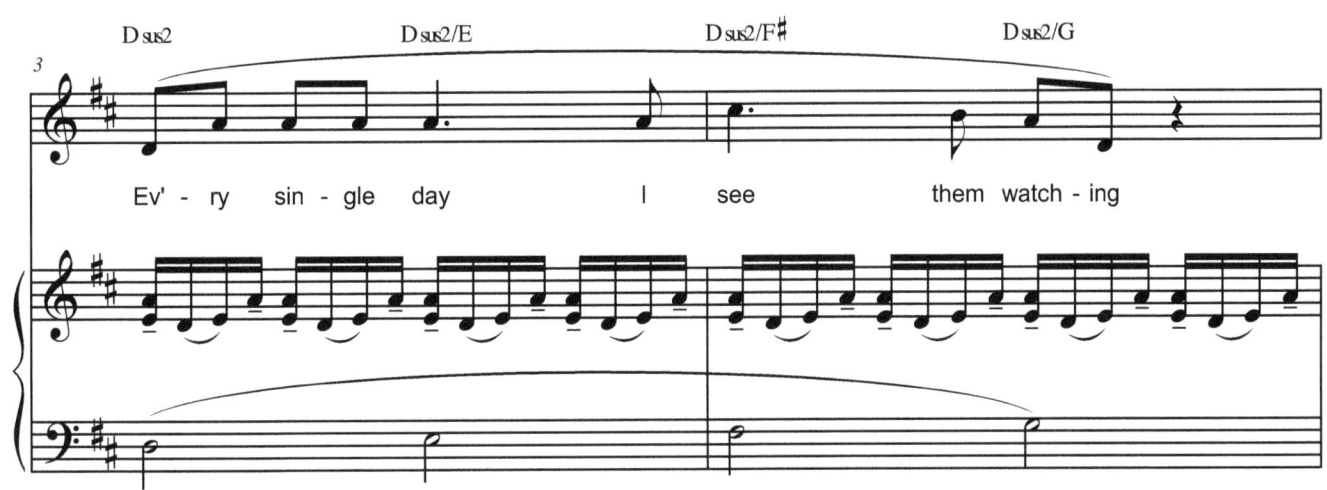

44

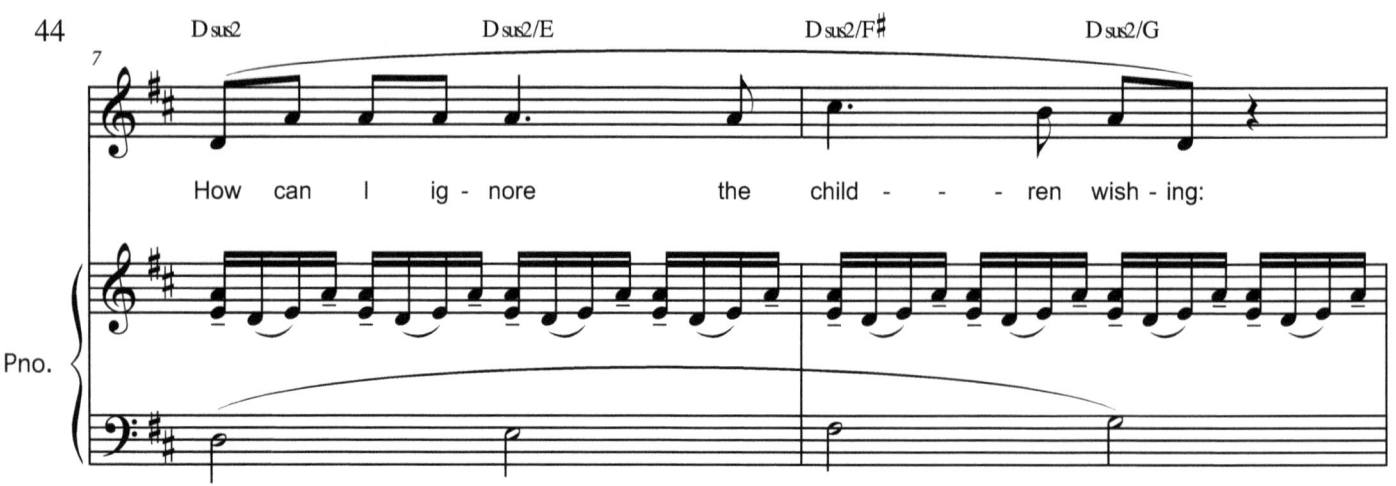

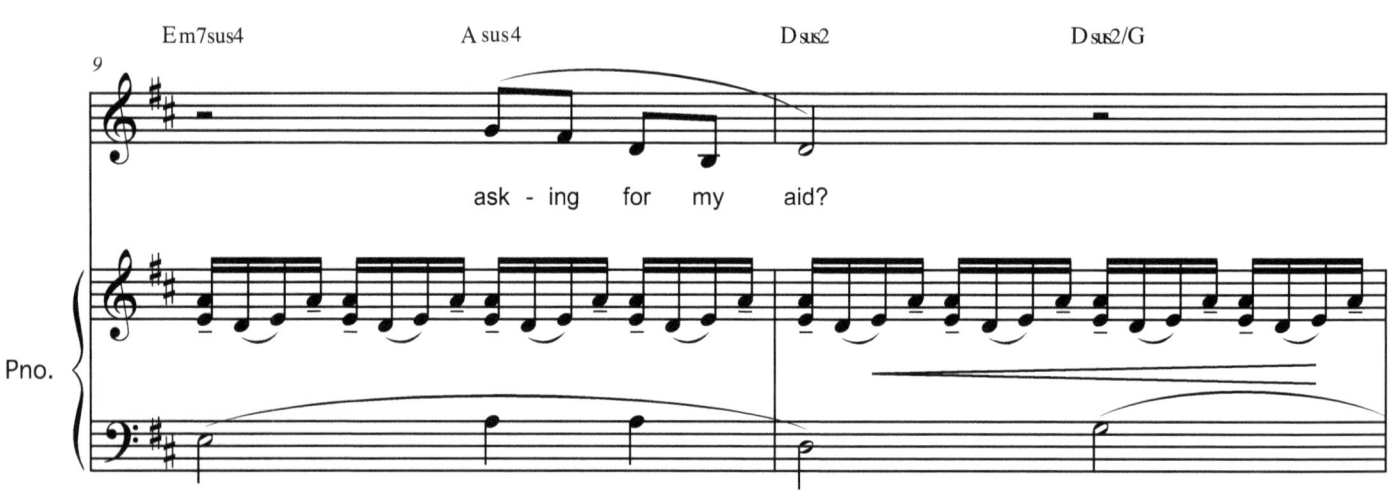

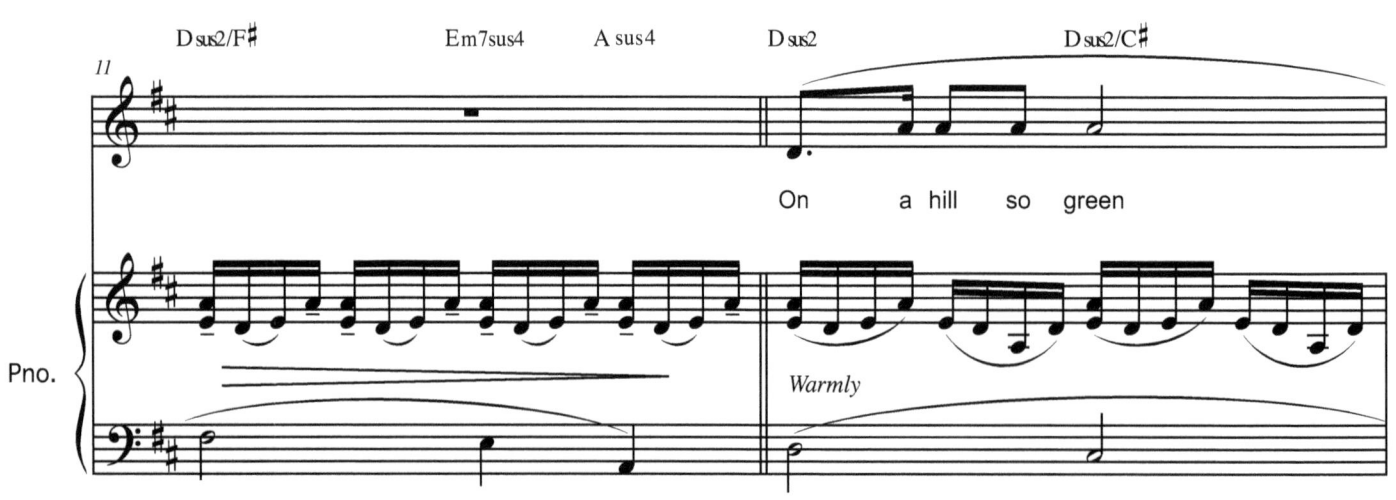

The Railway Children p 2/8

45

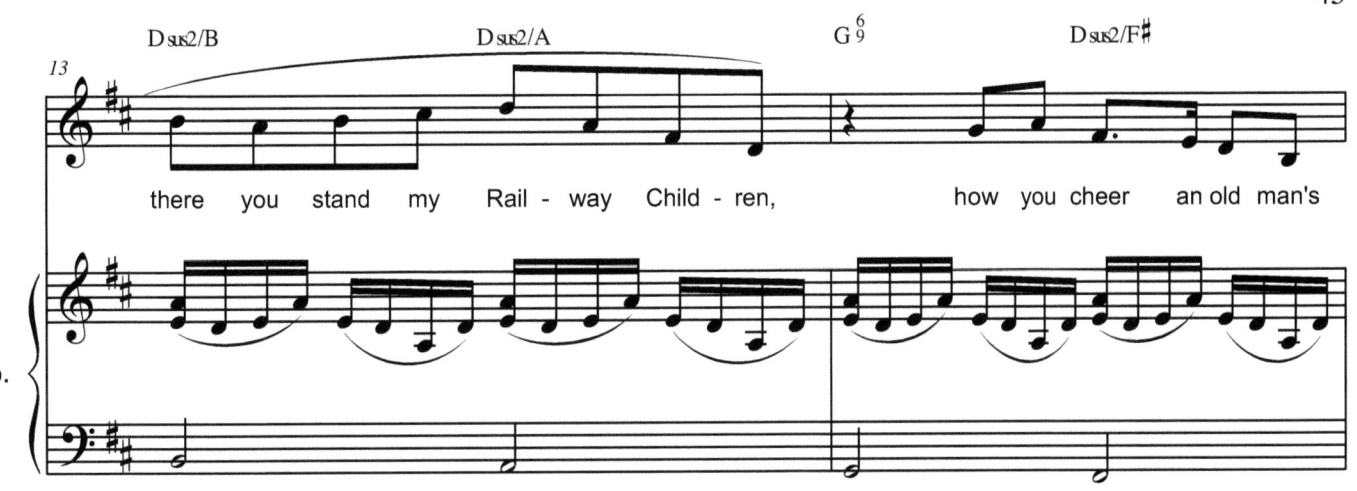

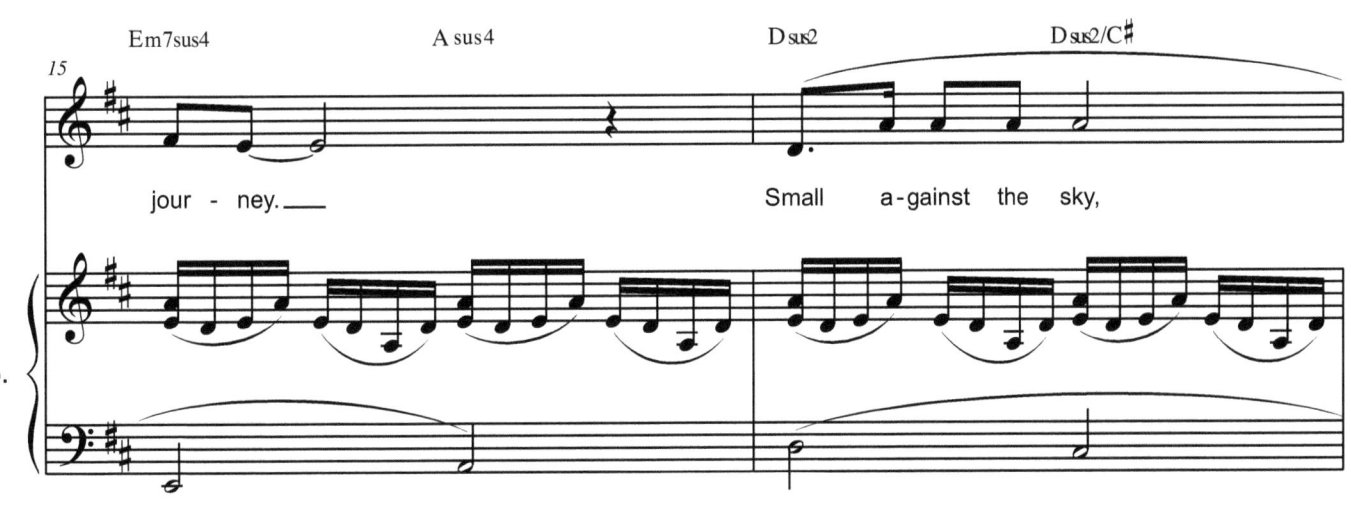

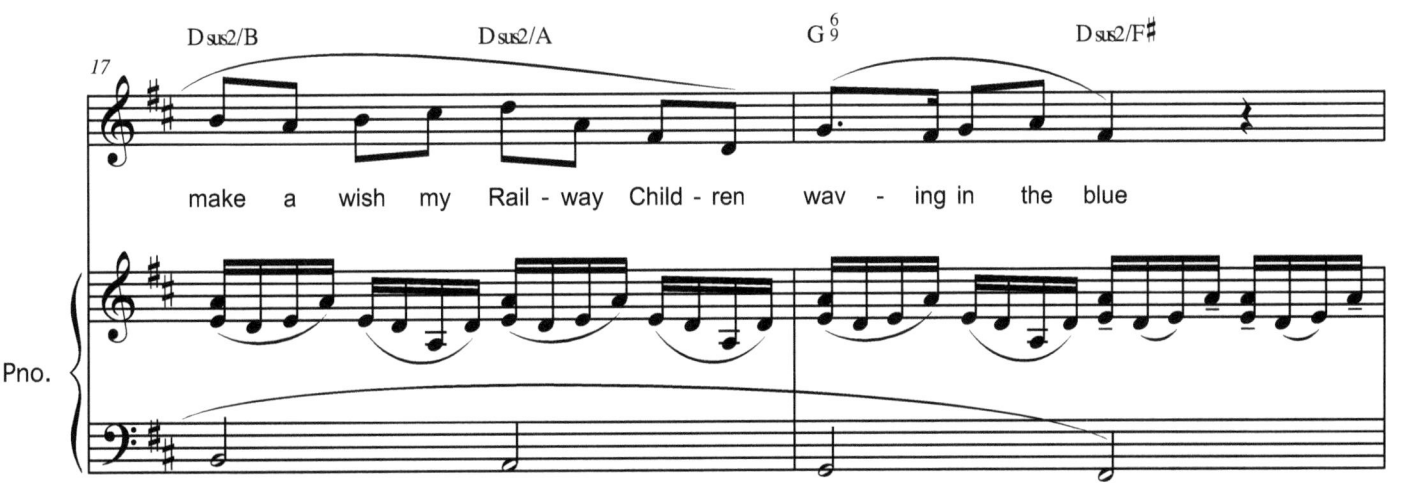

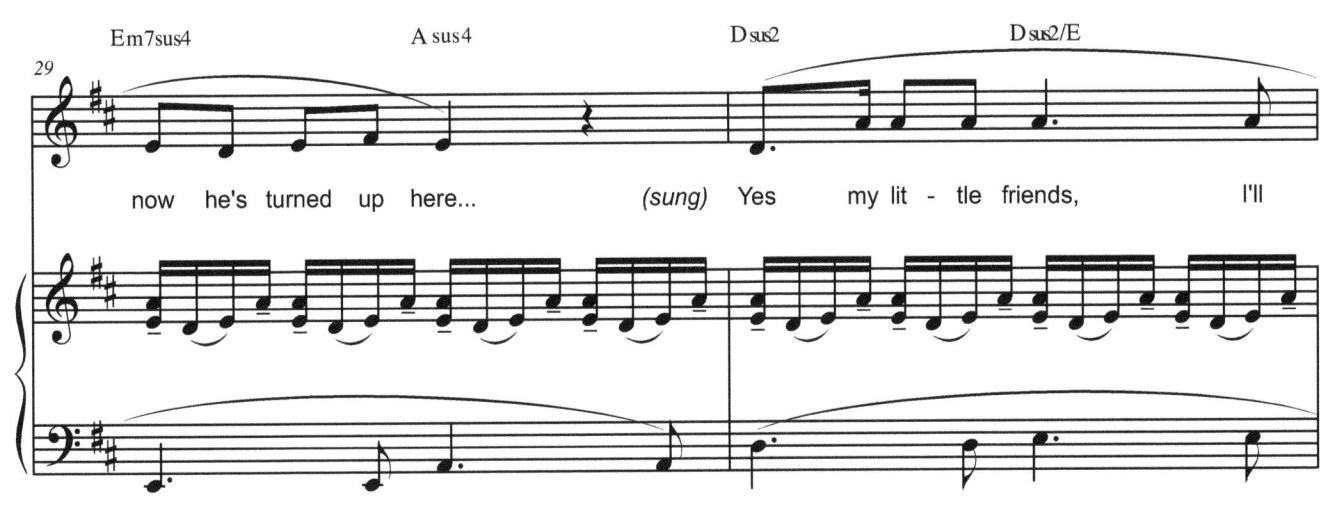

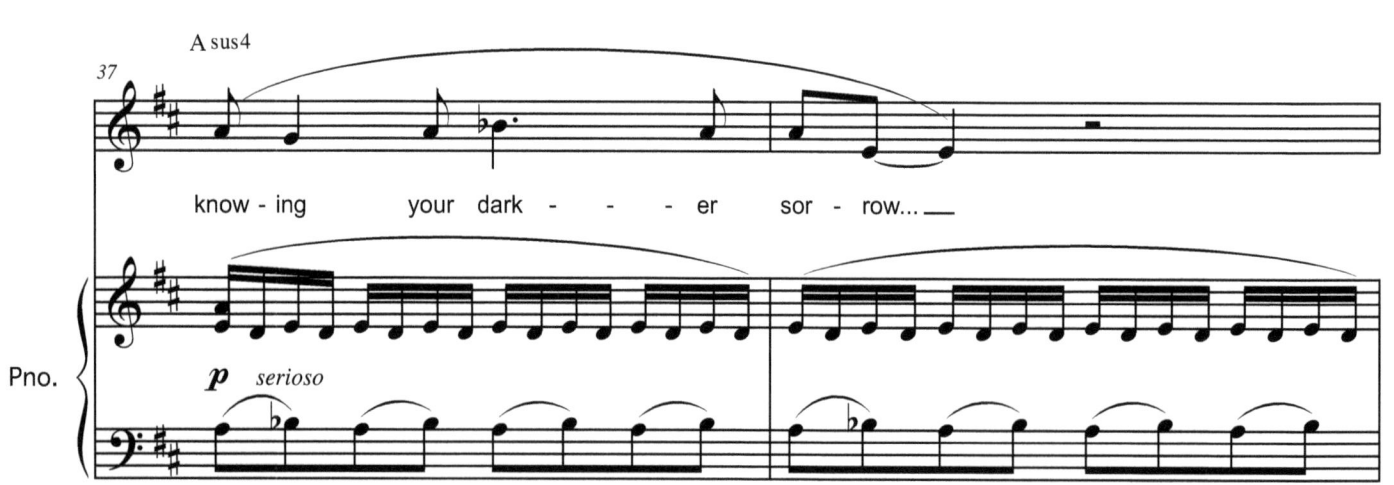

D♭(add2)
Cm7
A♭m6/C♭
E♭(add2)/B♭
E♭(add2)/G
47
watch me wave to you, make a wish and wave
Pno.
Fm7sus4
B♭sus4
E♭sus2
49
Wish-es do come true...
Pno.
51
Pno.
8va
mp
53
Pno.
(8va)
morendo
niente

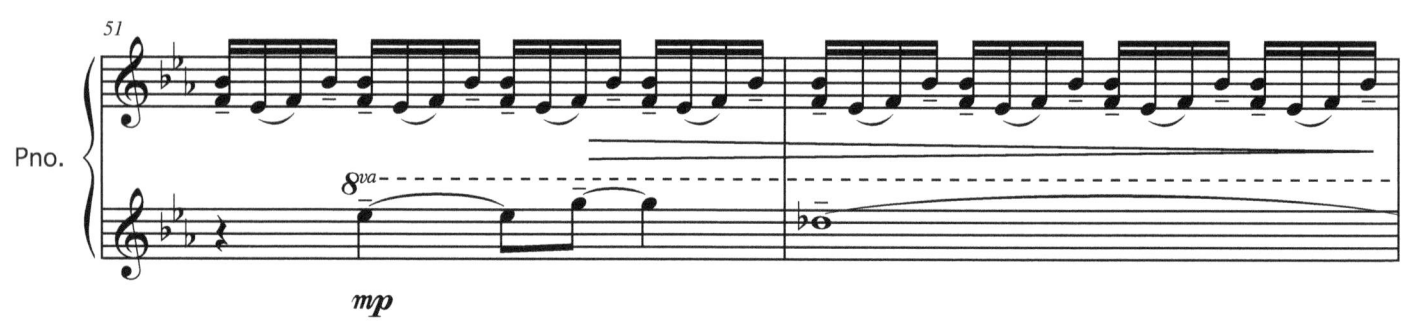

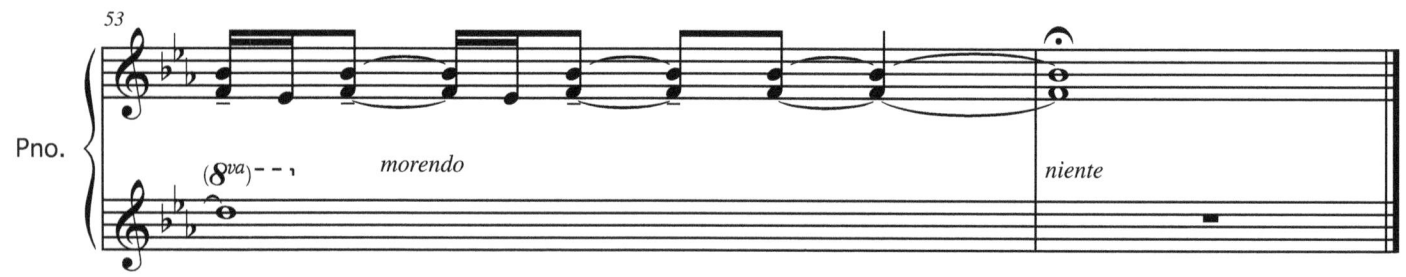

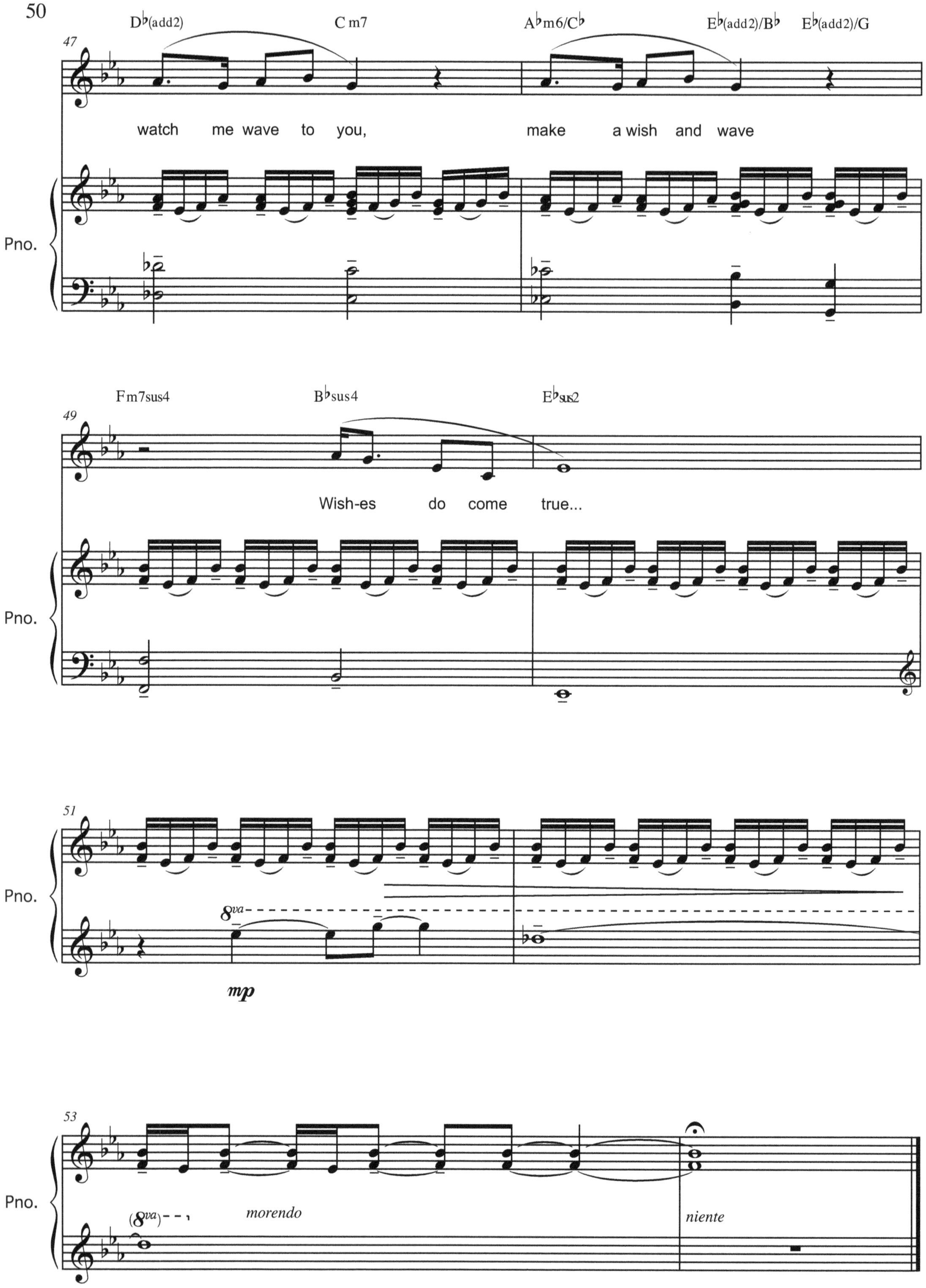

'Til The Day
The Railway Children

Lyrics by Julian Woolford

Music by Richard John

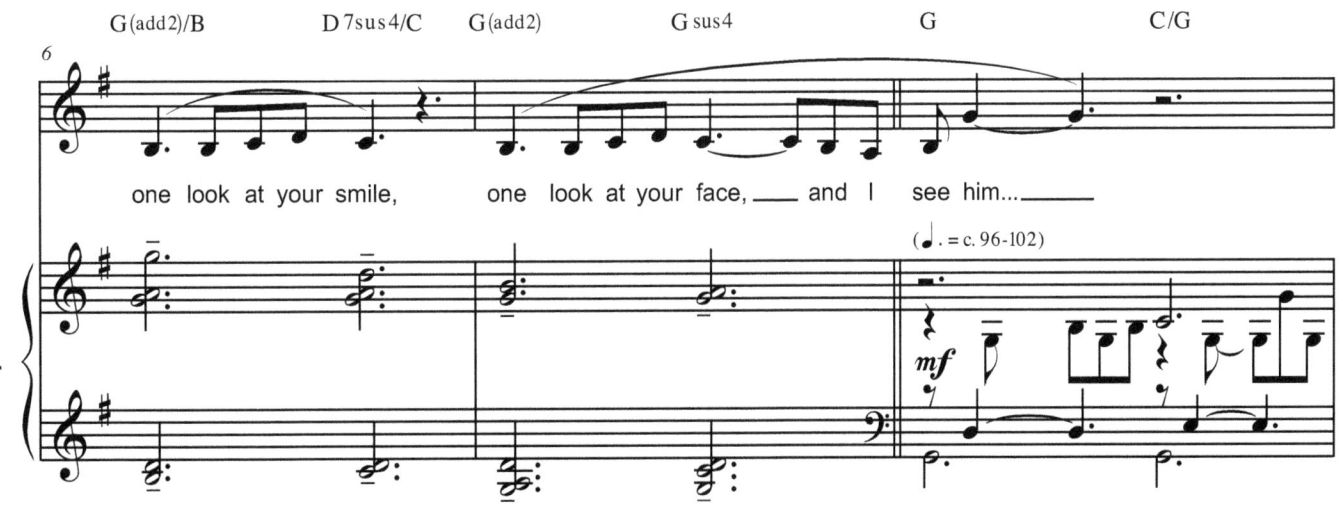

'Til The Day p 1/13

Copyright © Woolford & John 2007
International Copyright Secured. All Rights Reserved.

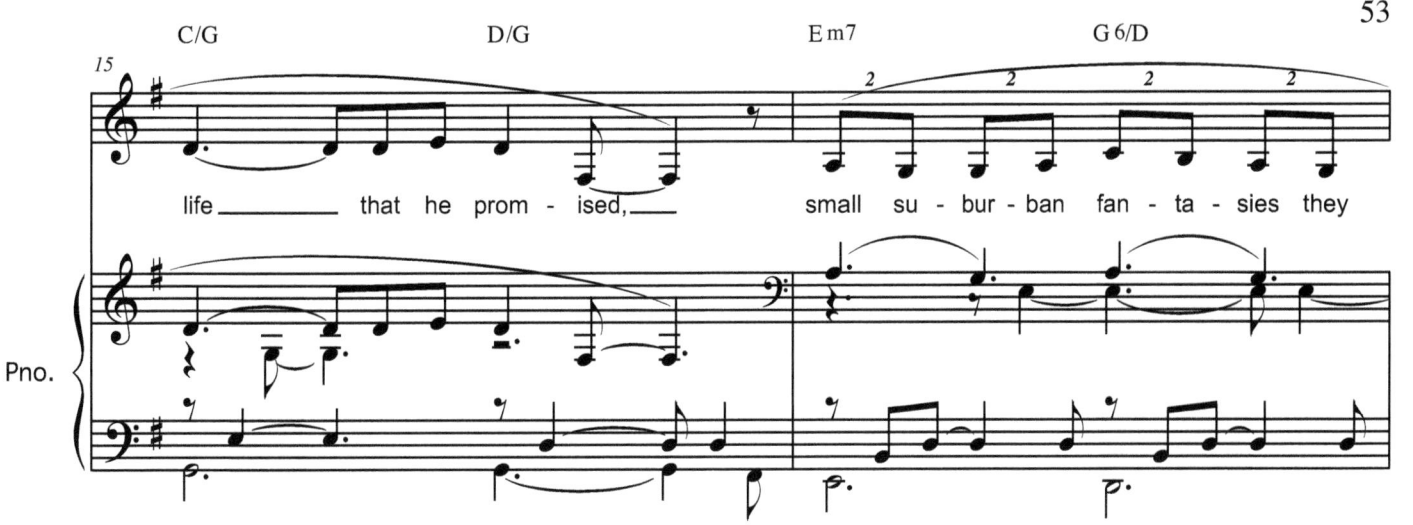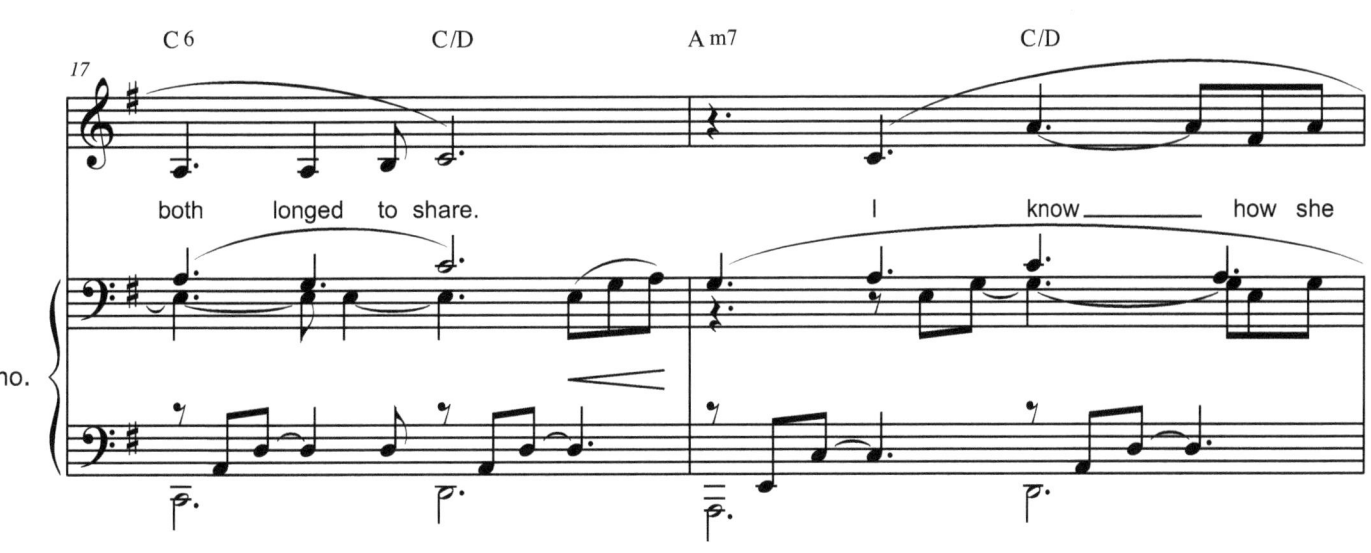

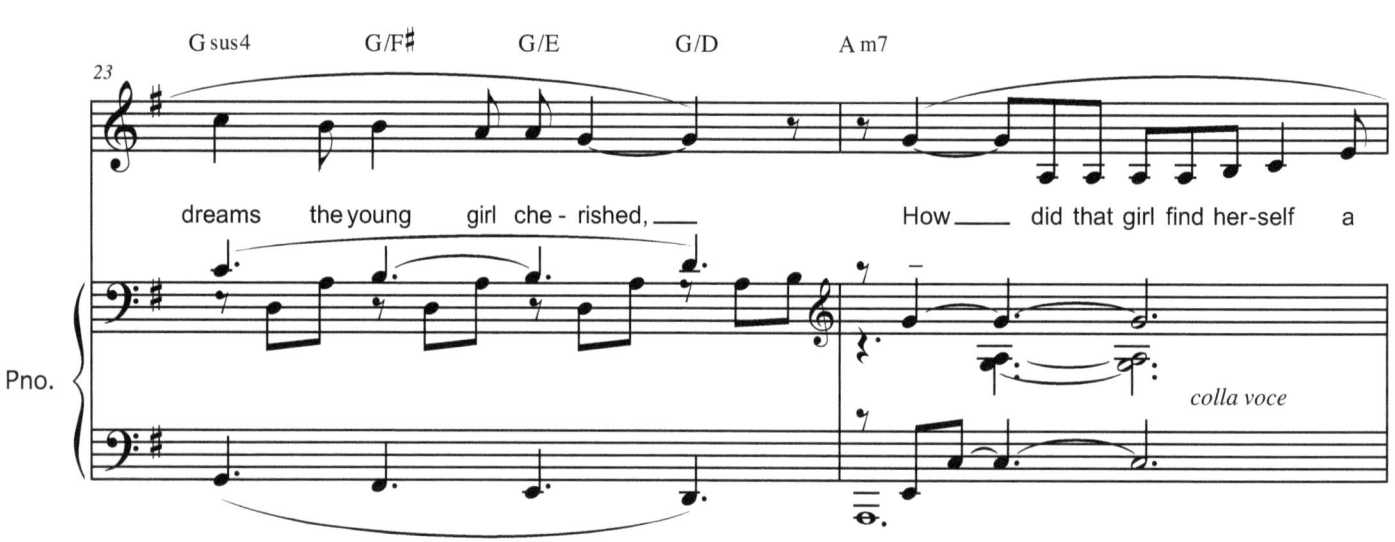

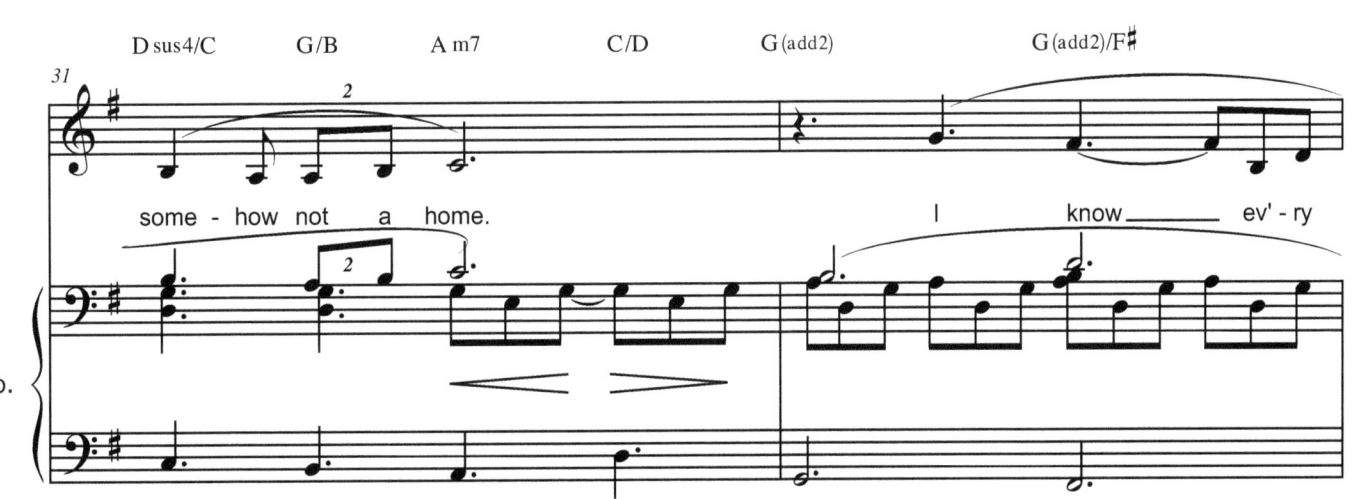

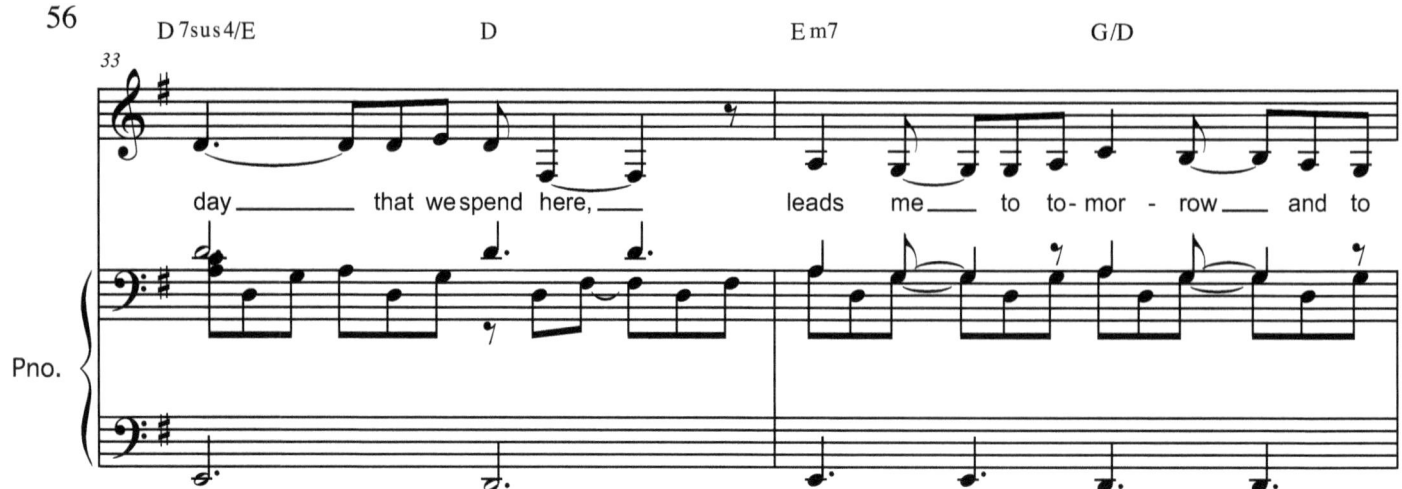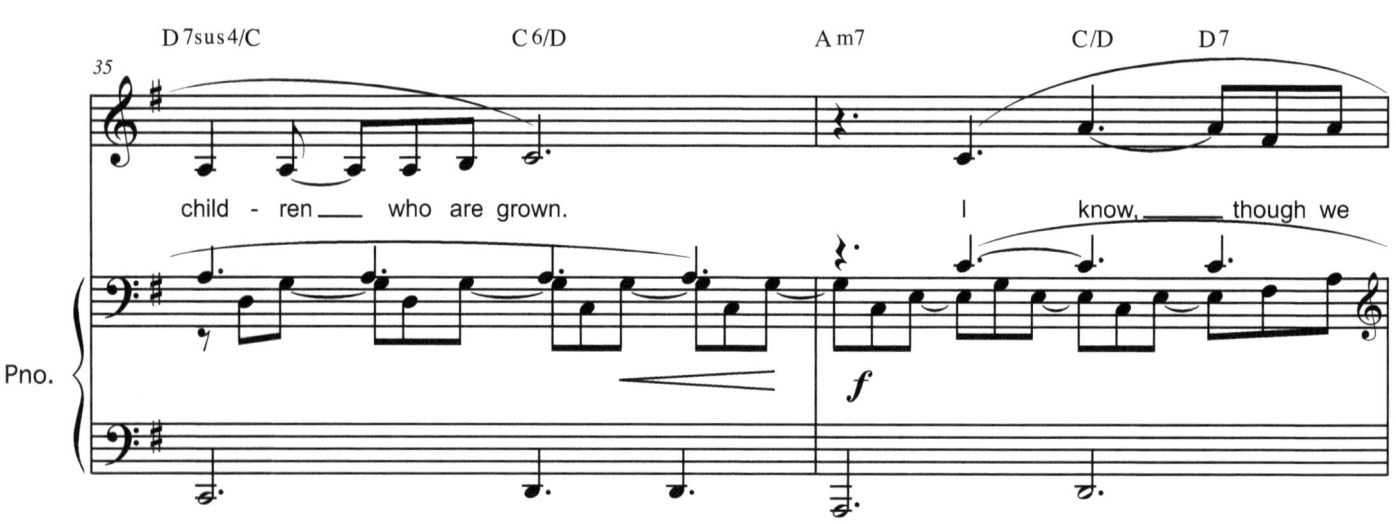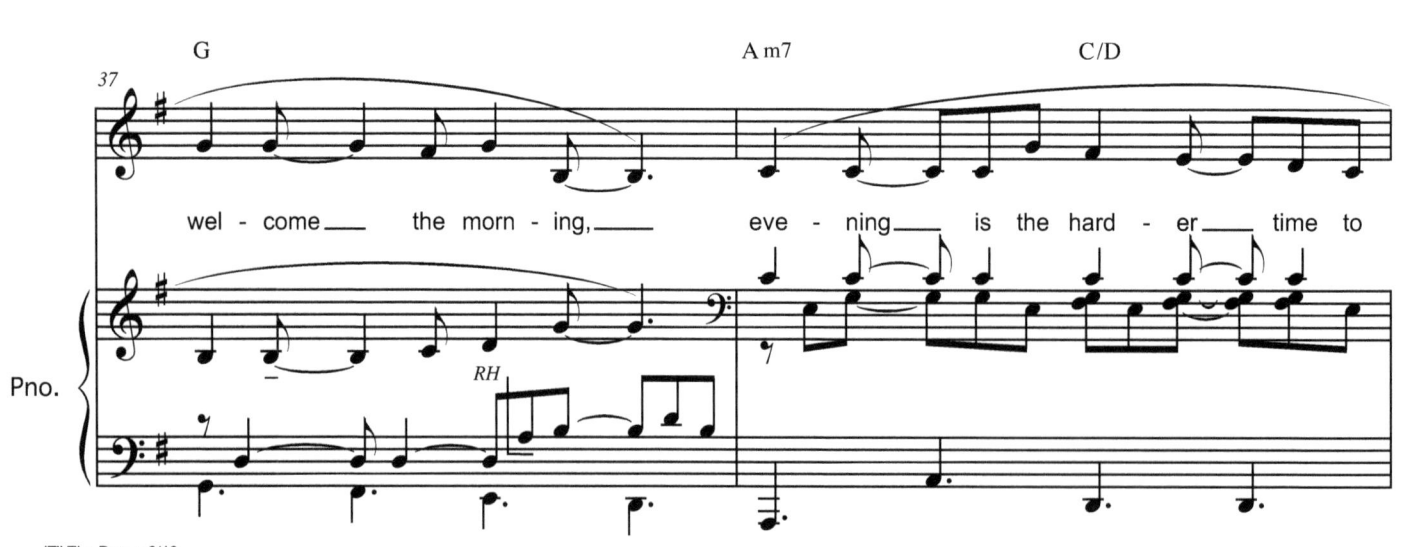

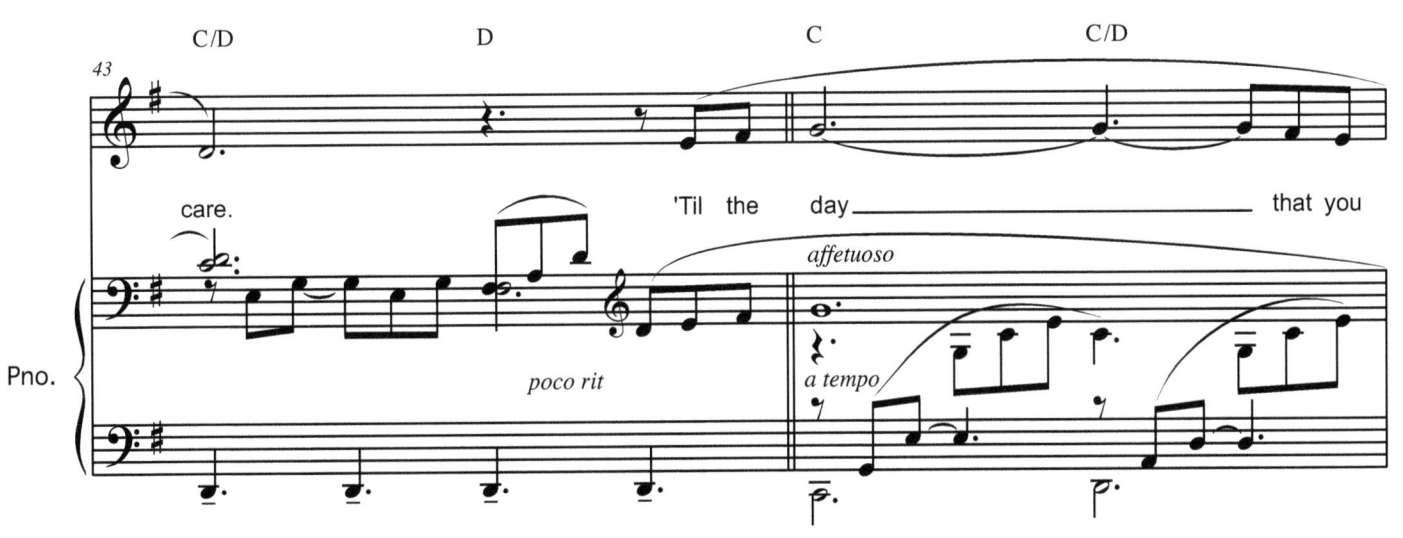

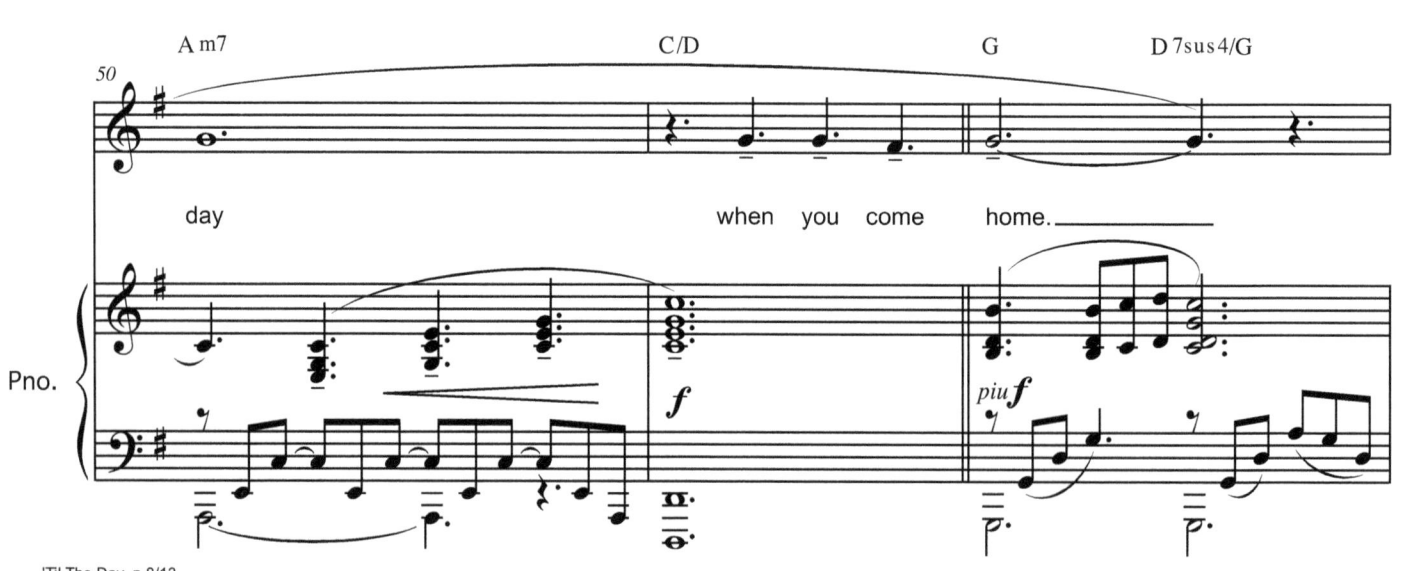

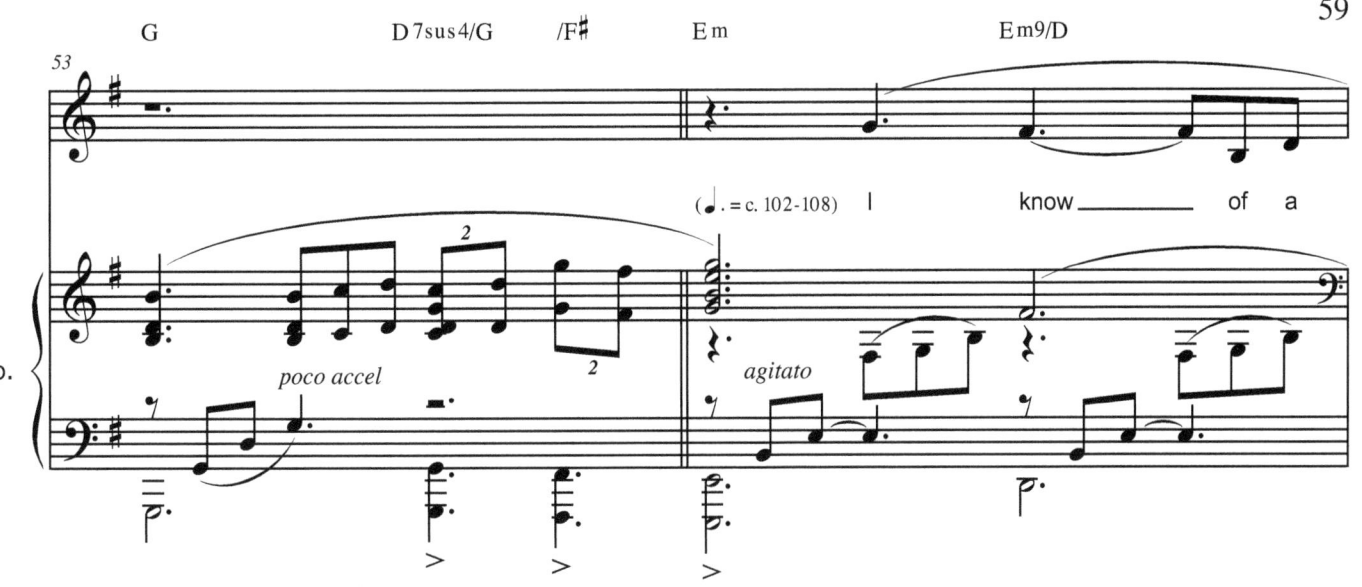
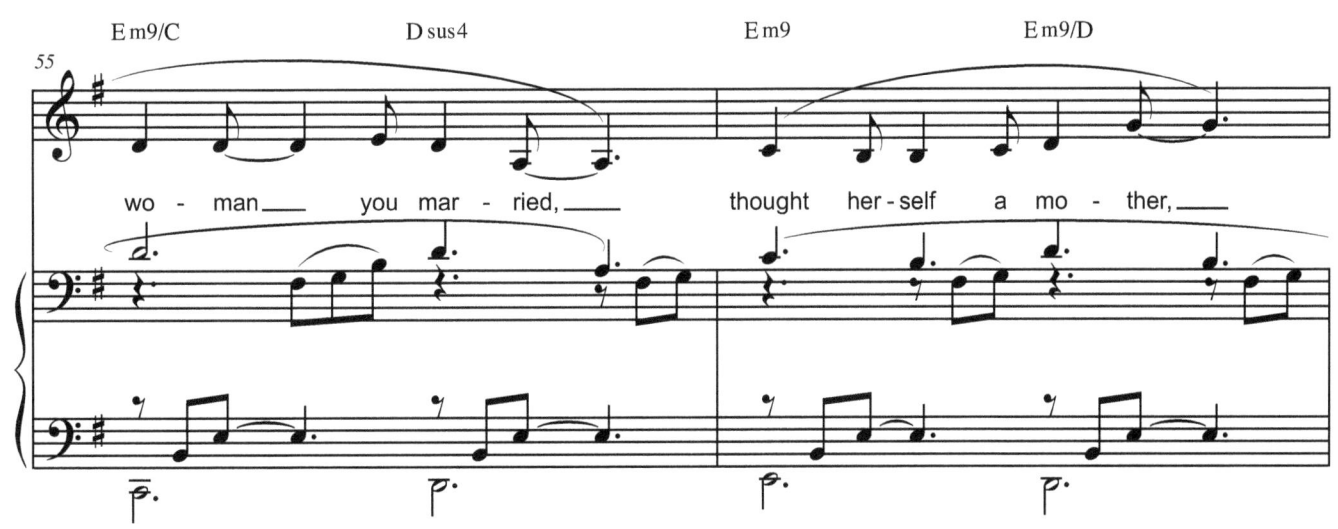
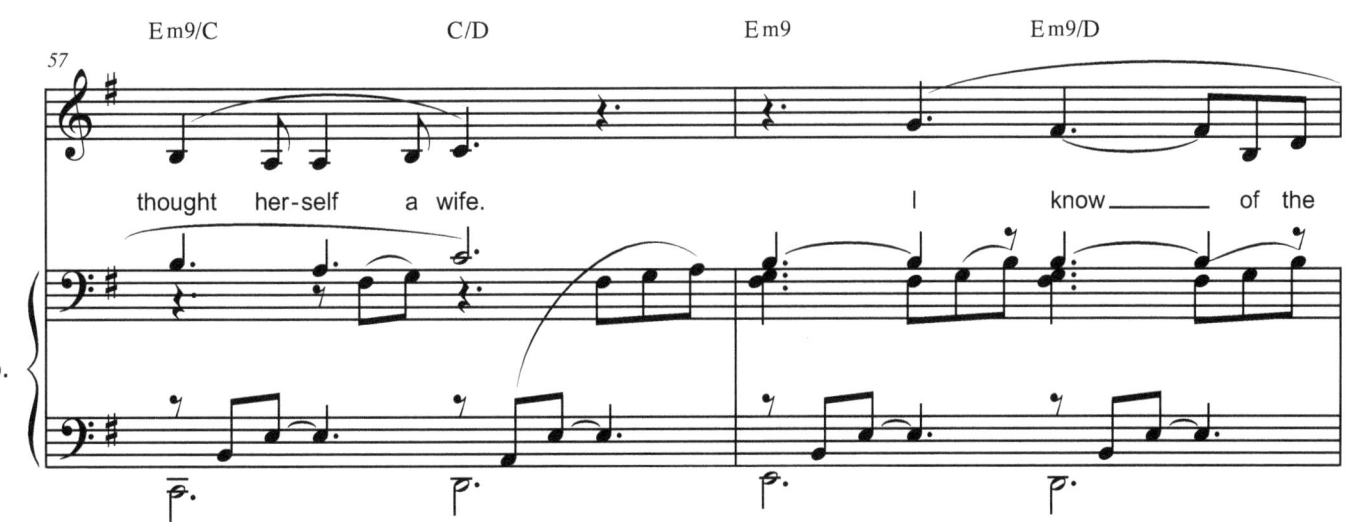

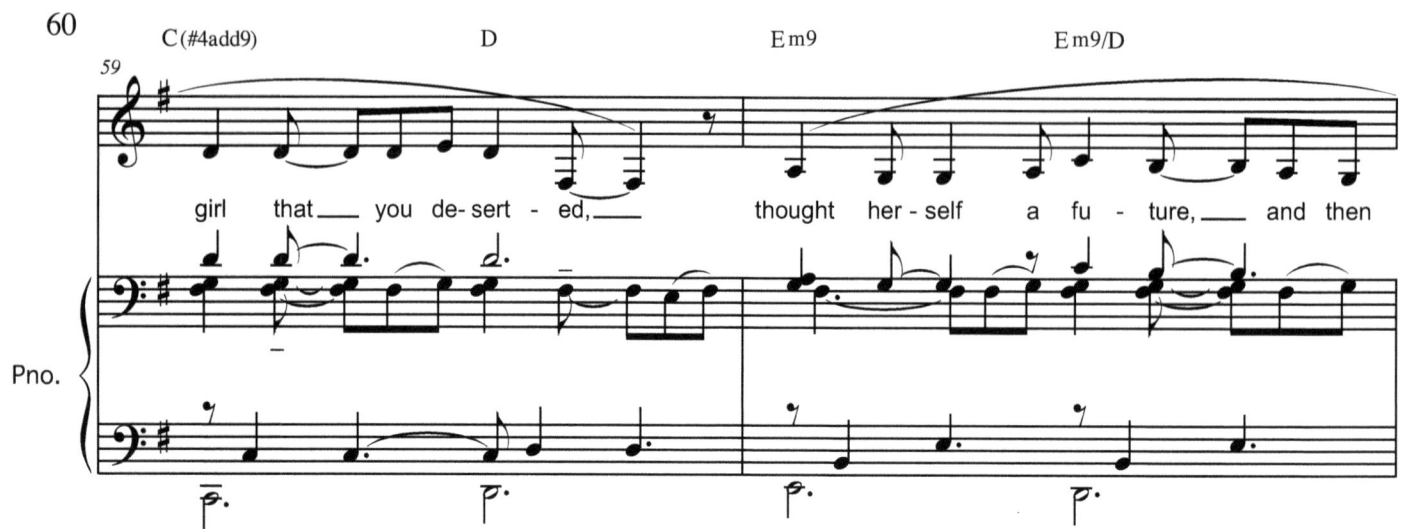
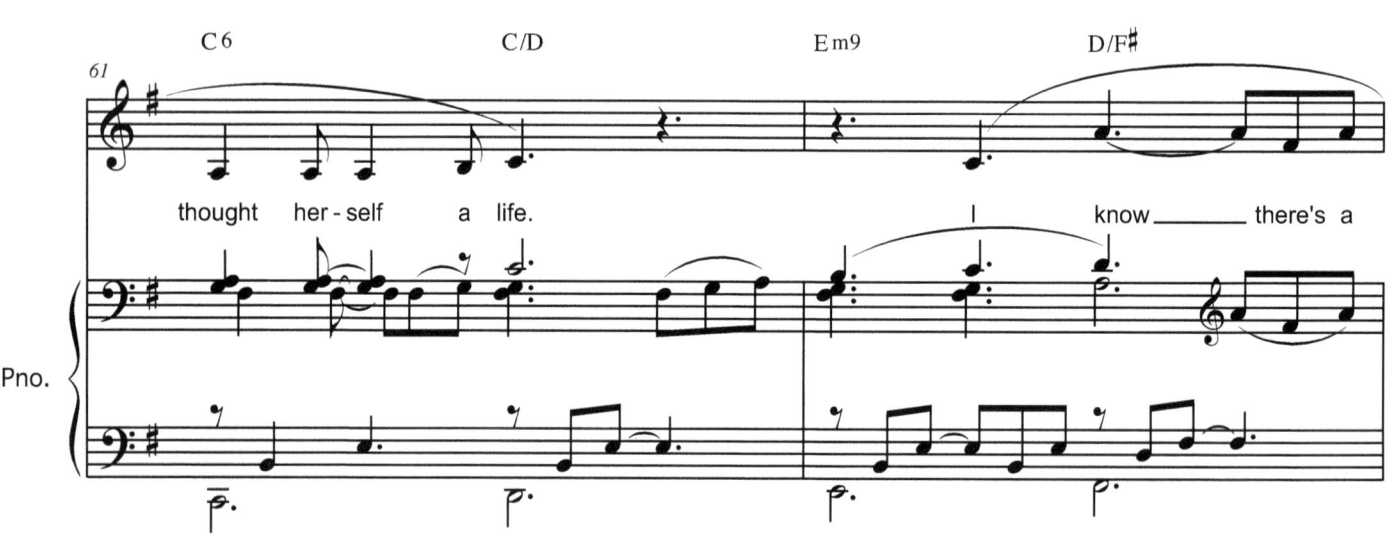
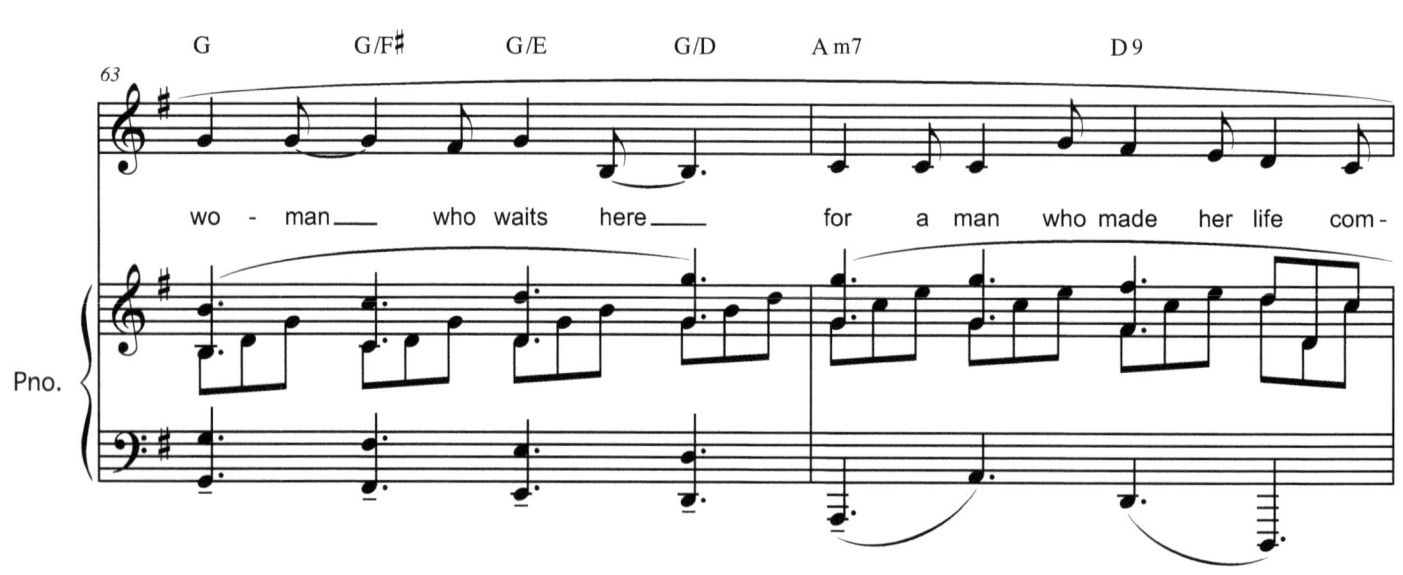

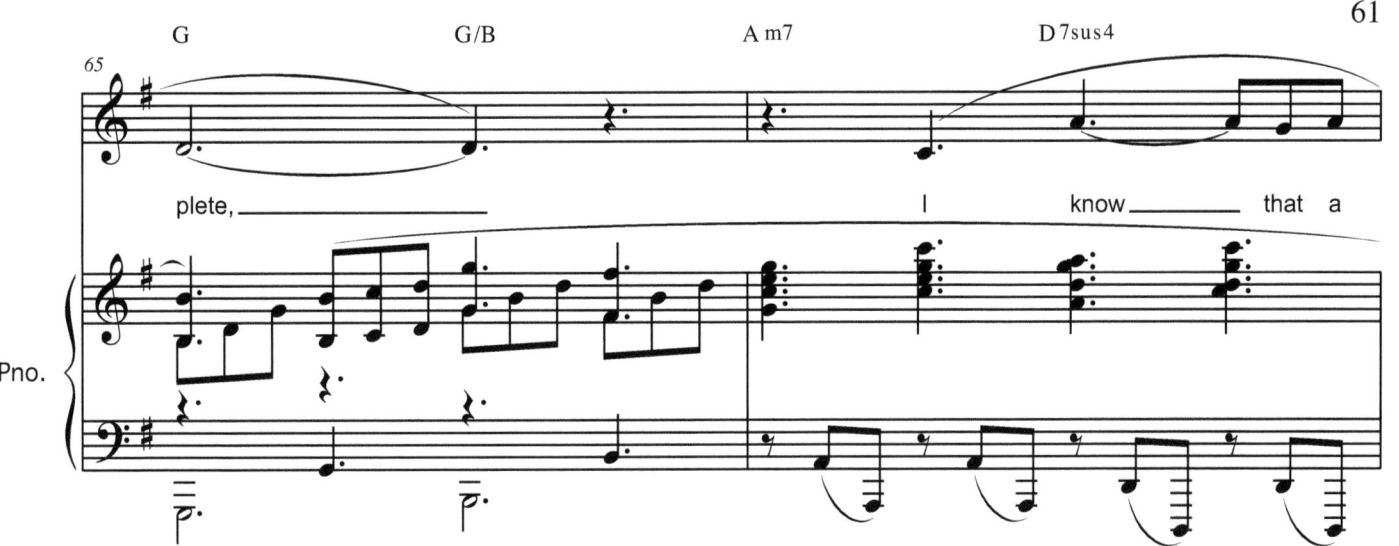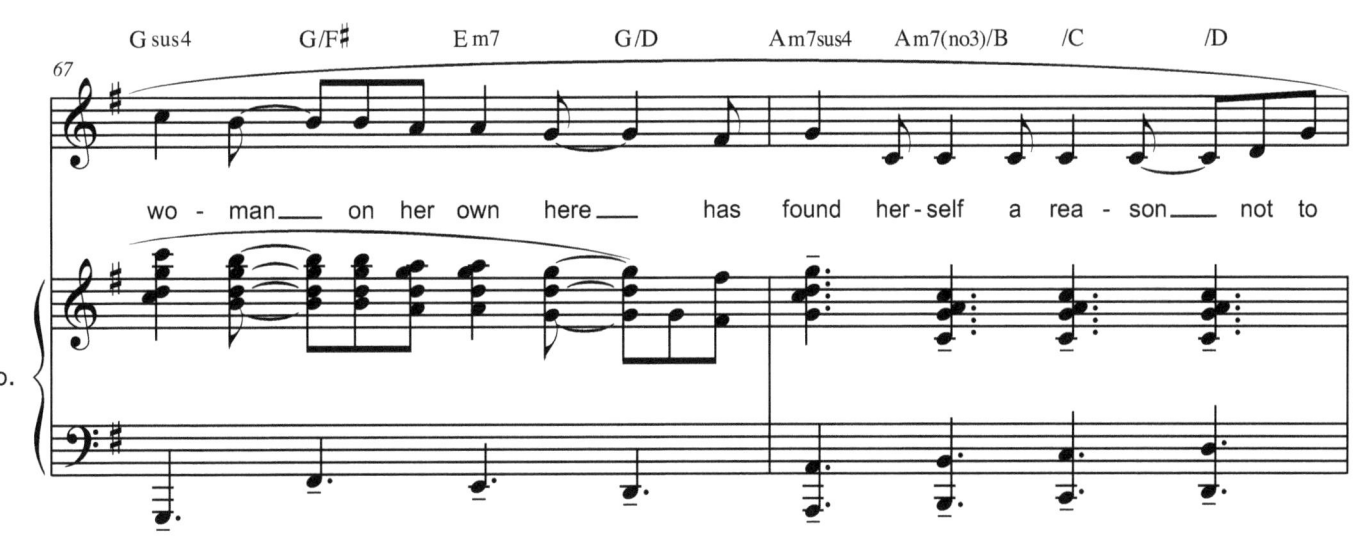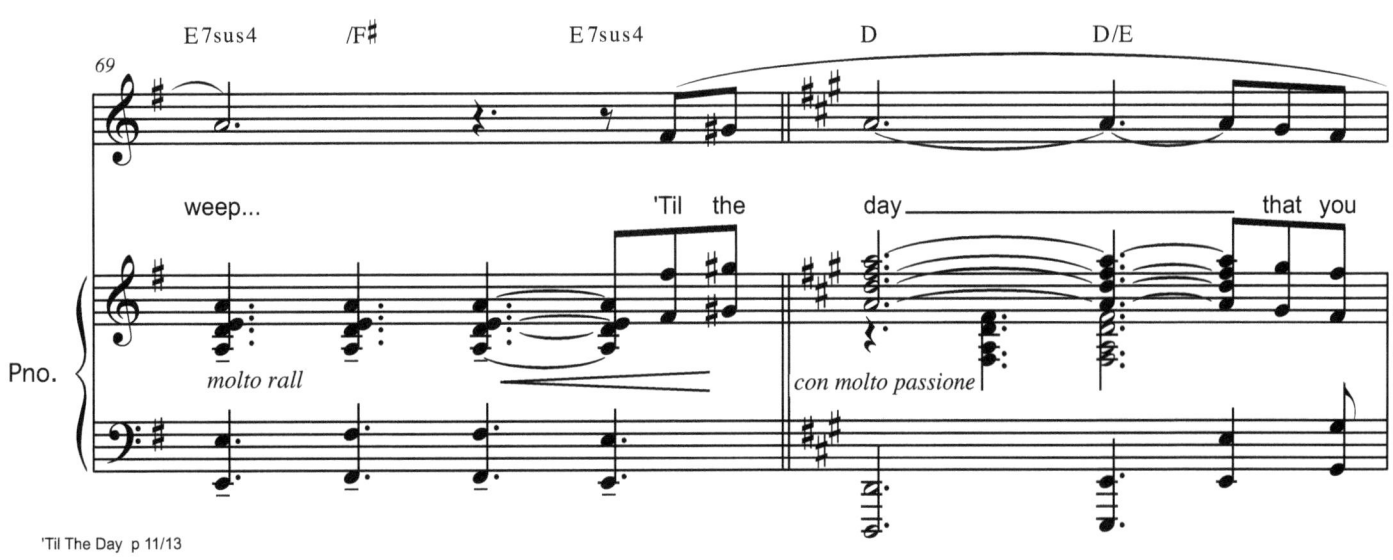

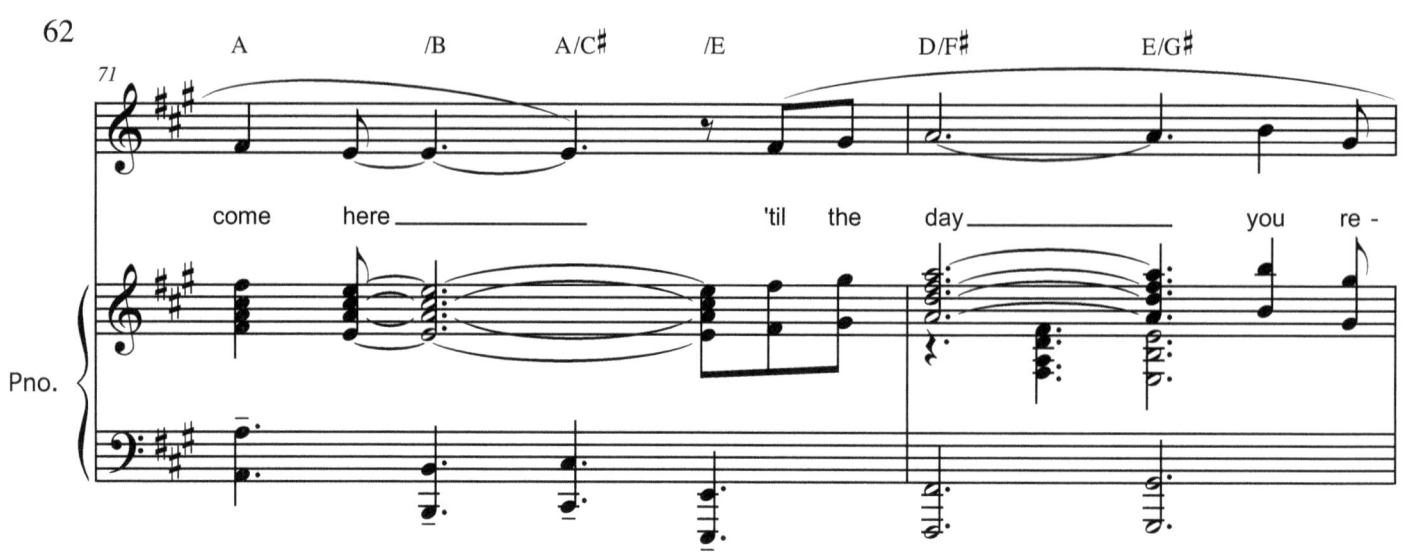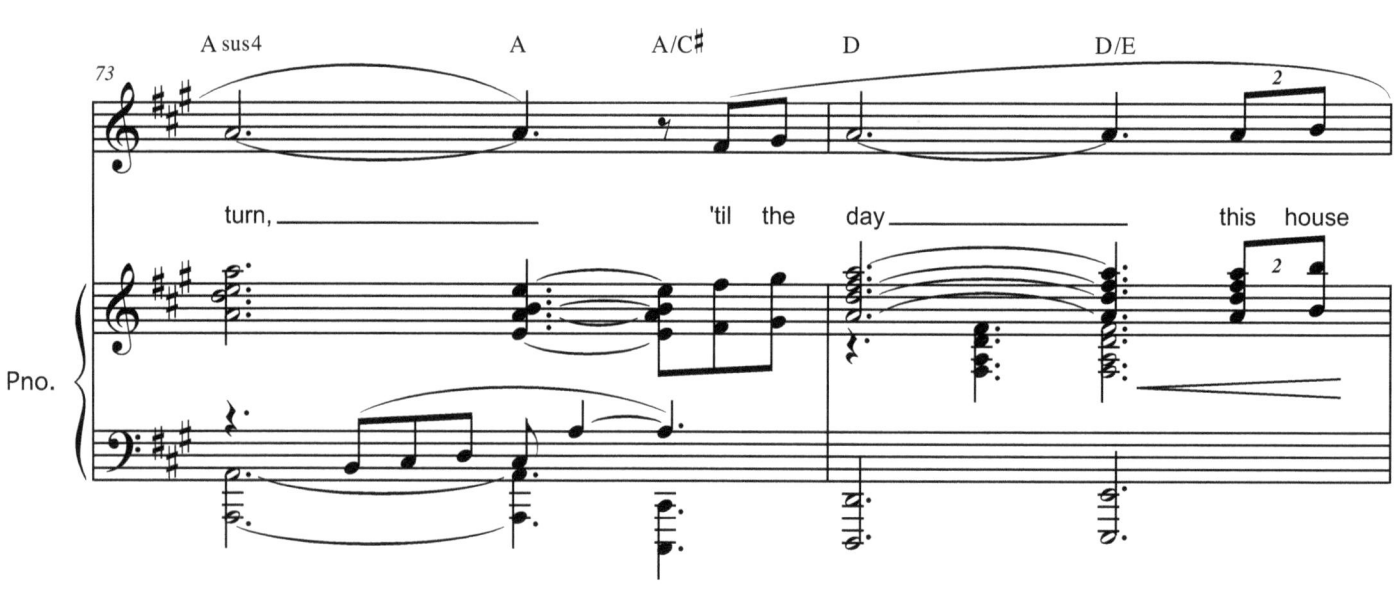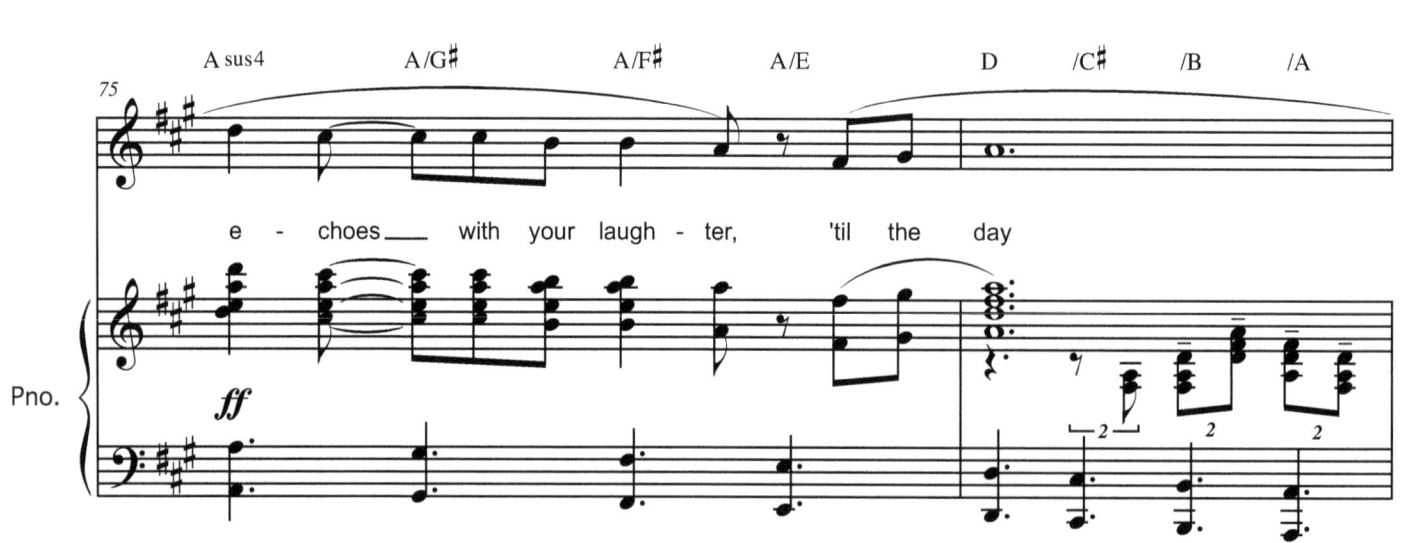

A Once In A Lifetime Day

Lyrics by Julian Woolford

The Railway Children

Music by Richard John

Once In A Lifetime Day p 12/21

Once In A Lifetime Day p 21/21

Busy Dreaming

The Railway Children

Lyrics by Julian Woolford

Music by Richard John

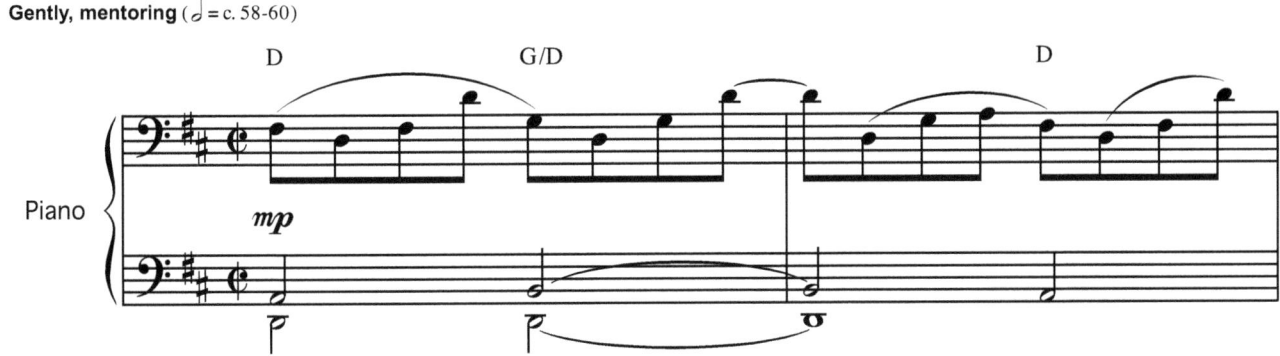

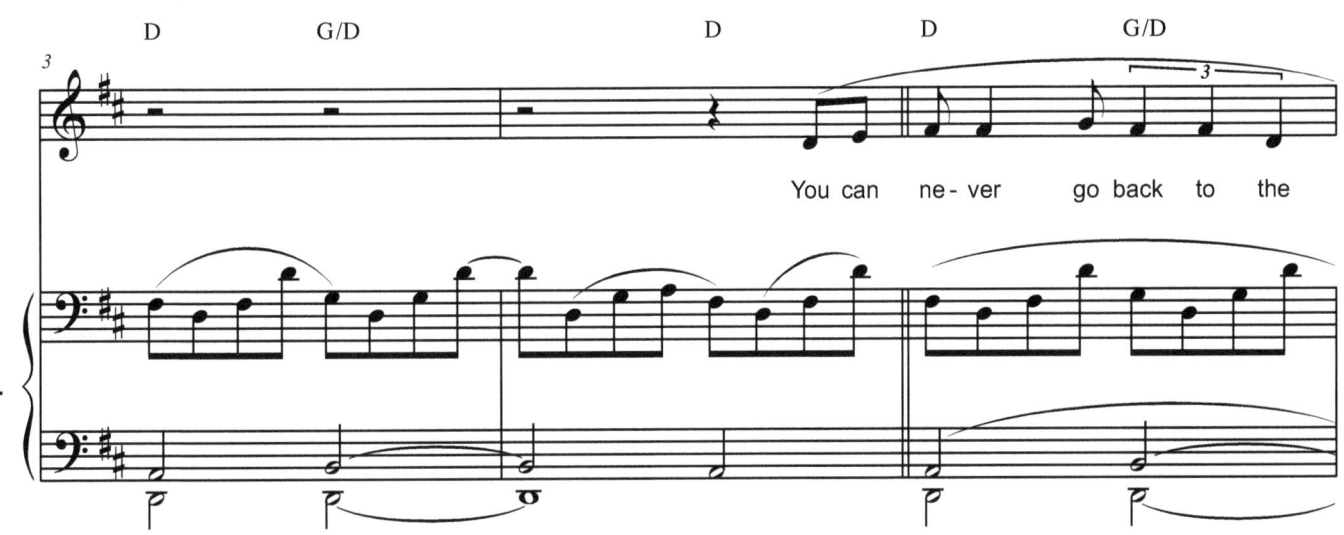

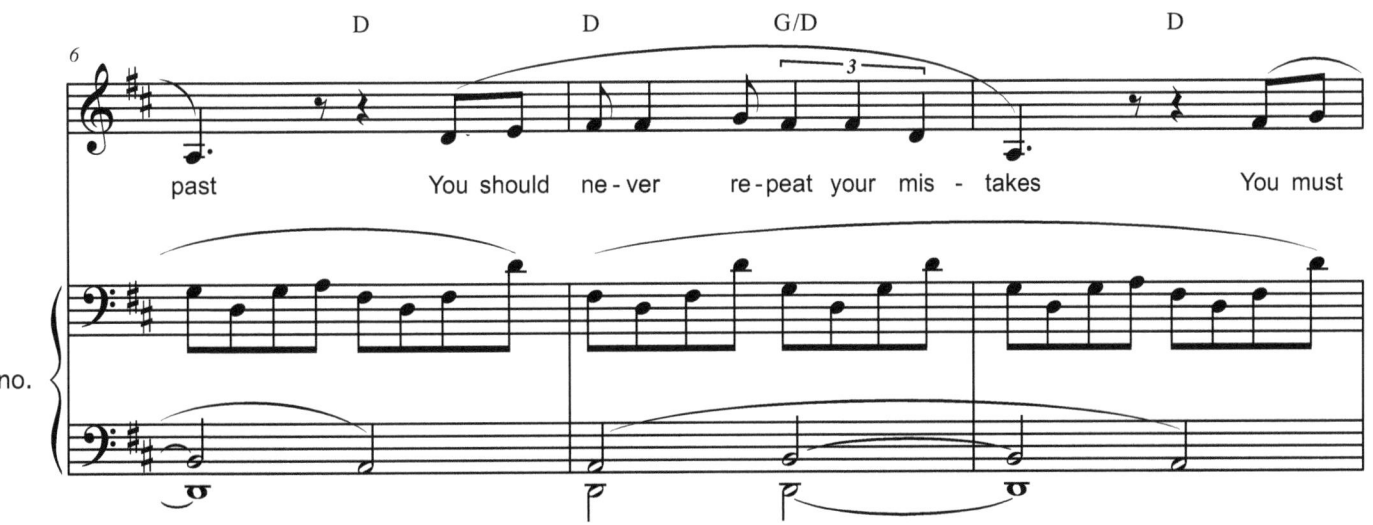

(While You're) Busy Dreaming p 1/8

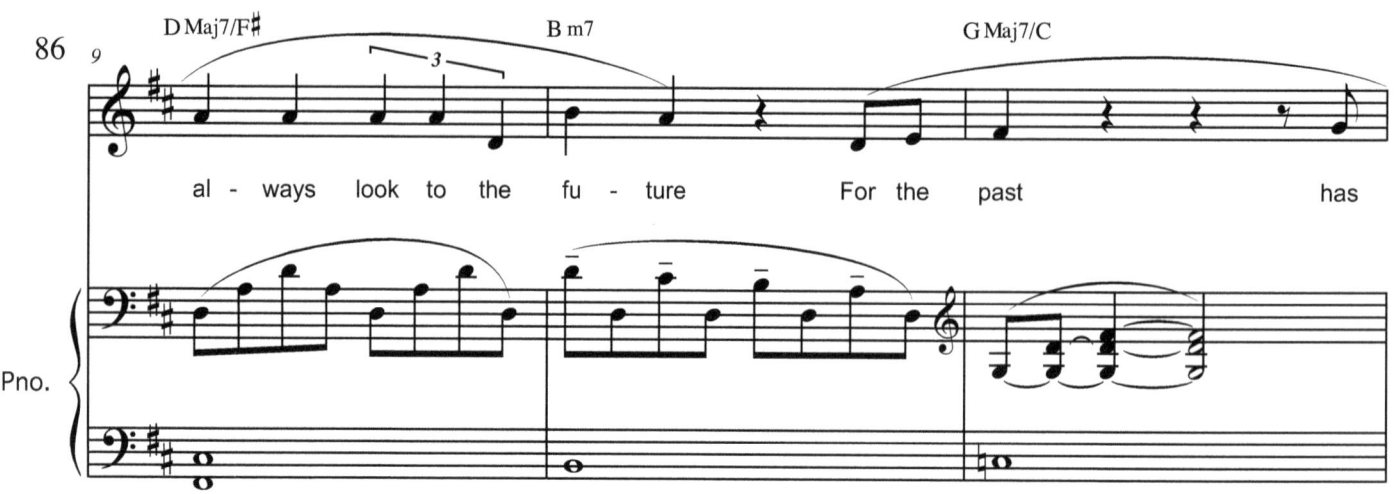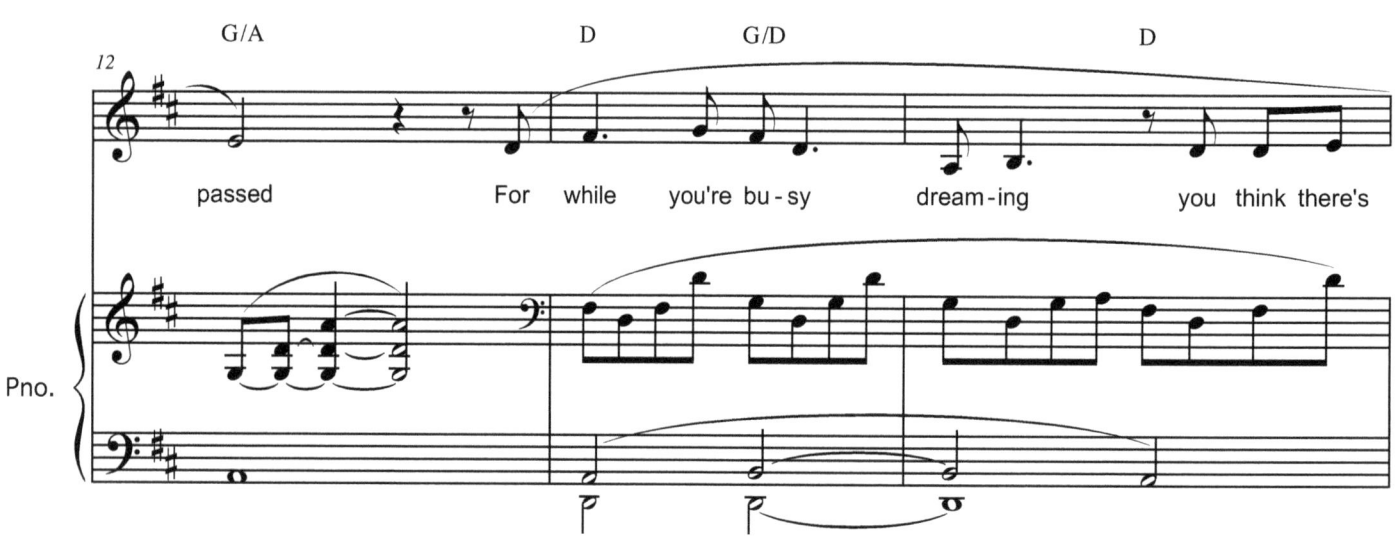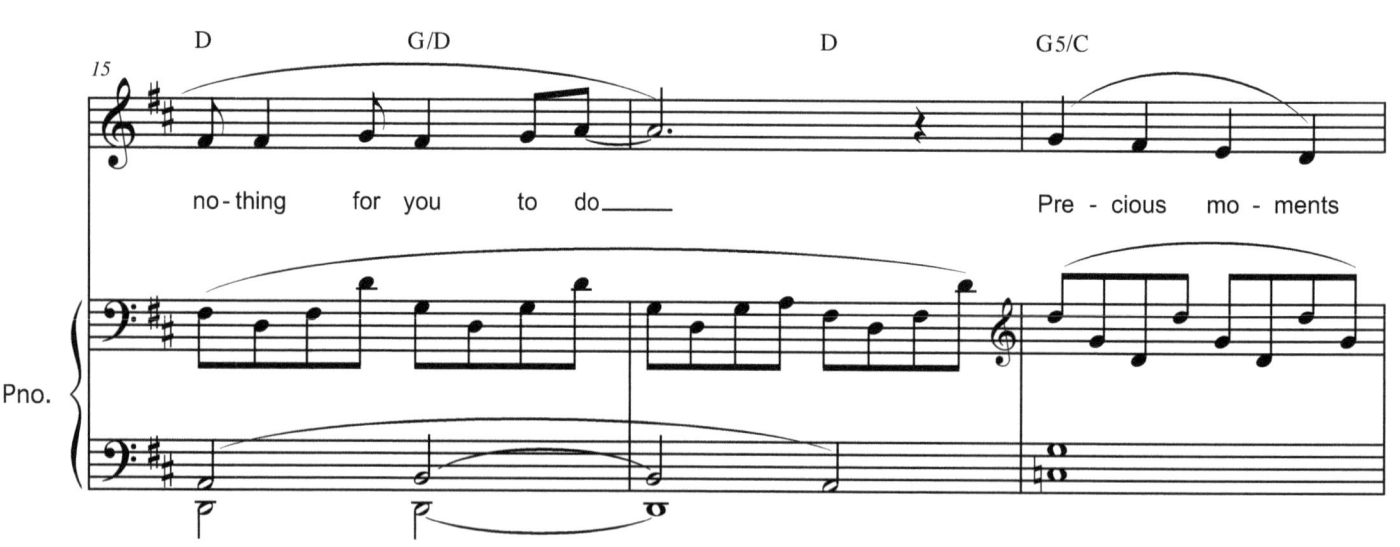

(While You're) Busy Dreaming p 2/8

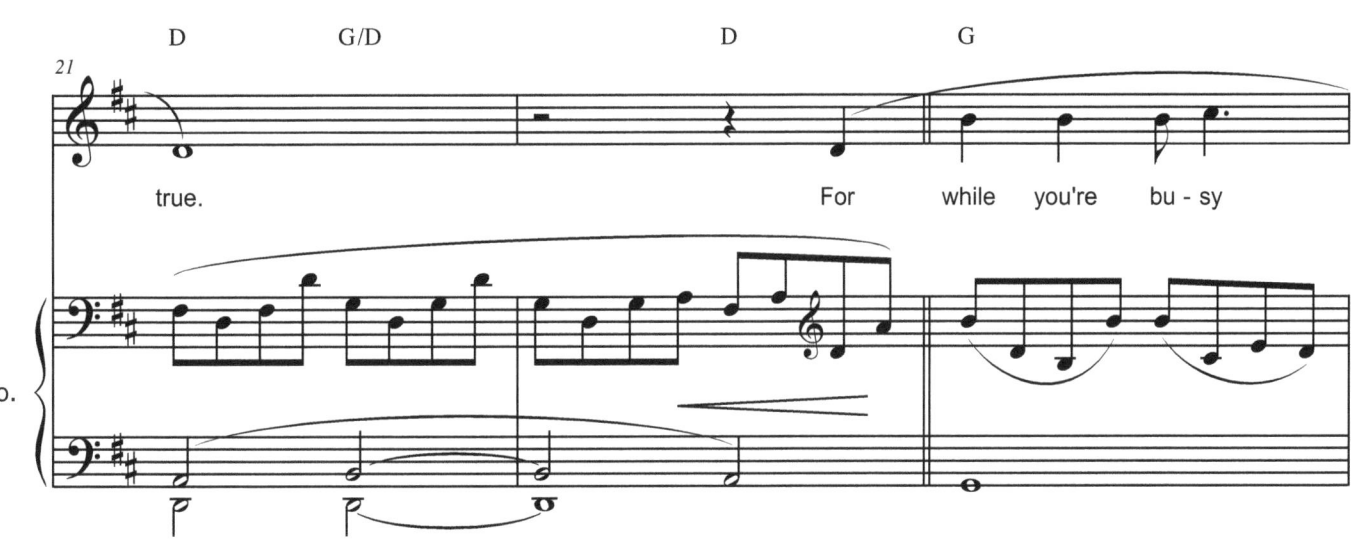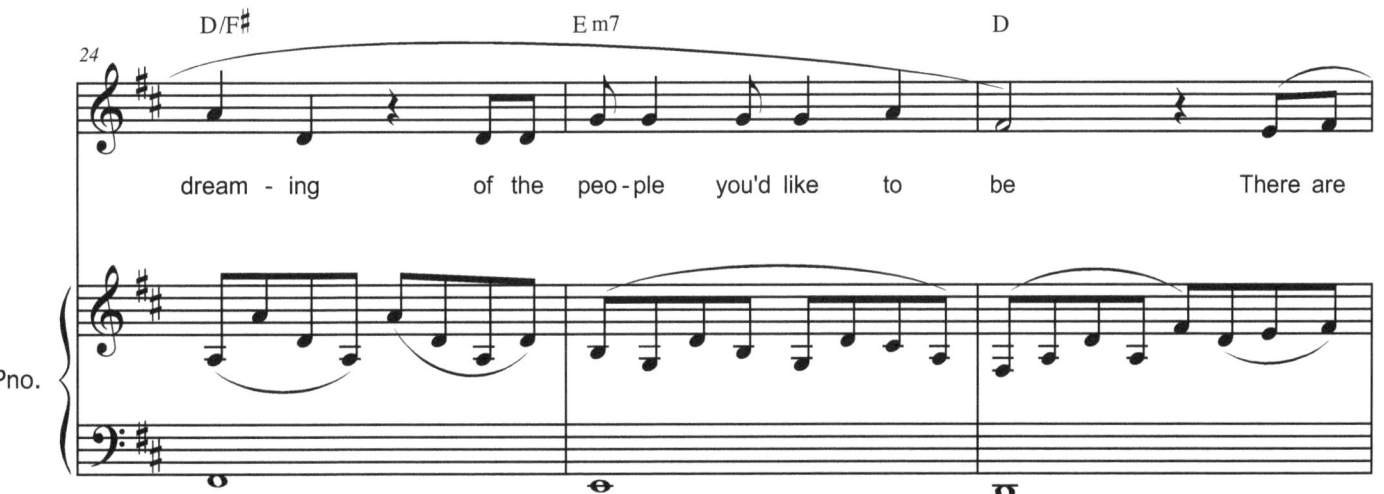

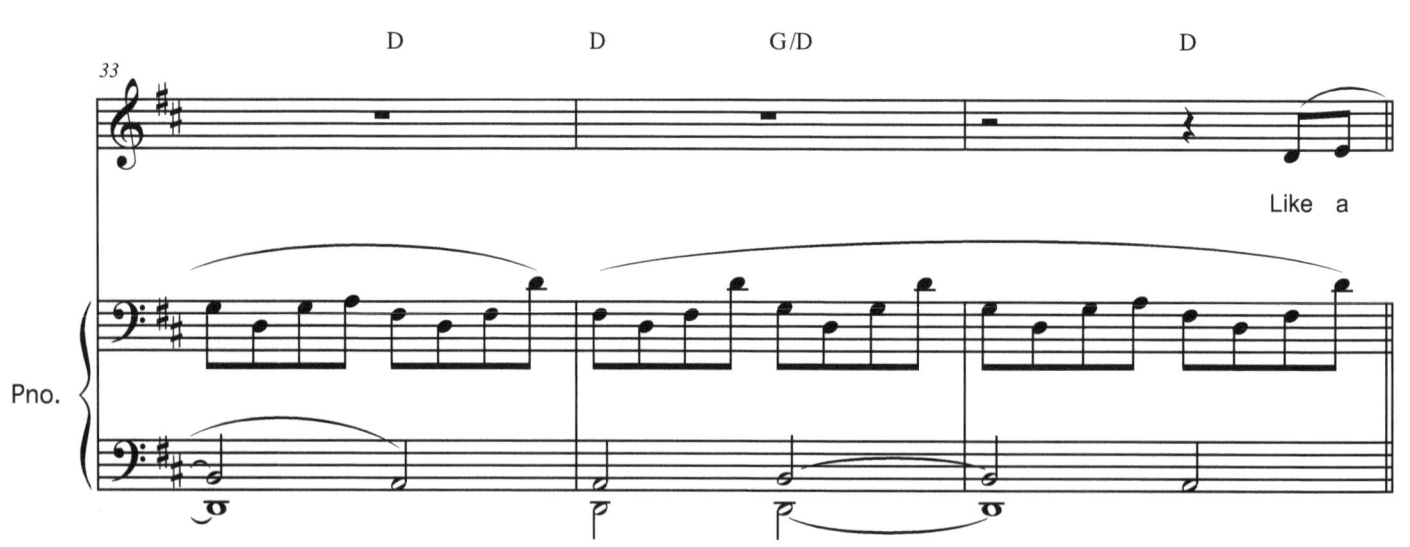

(While You're) Busy Dreaming p 4/8

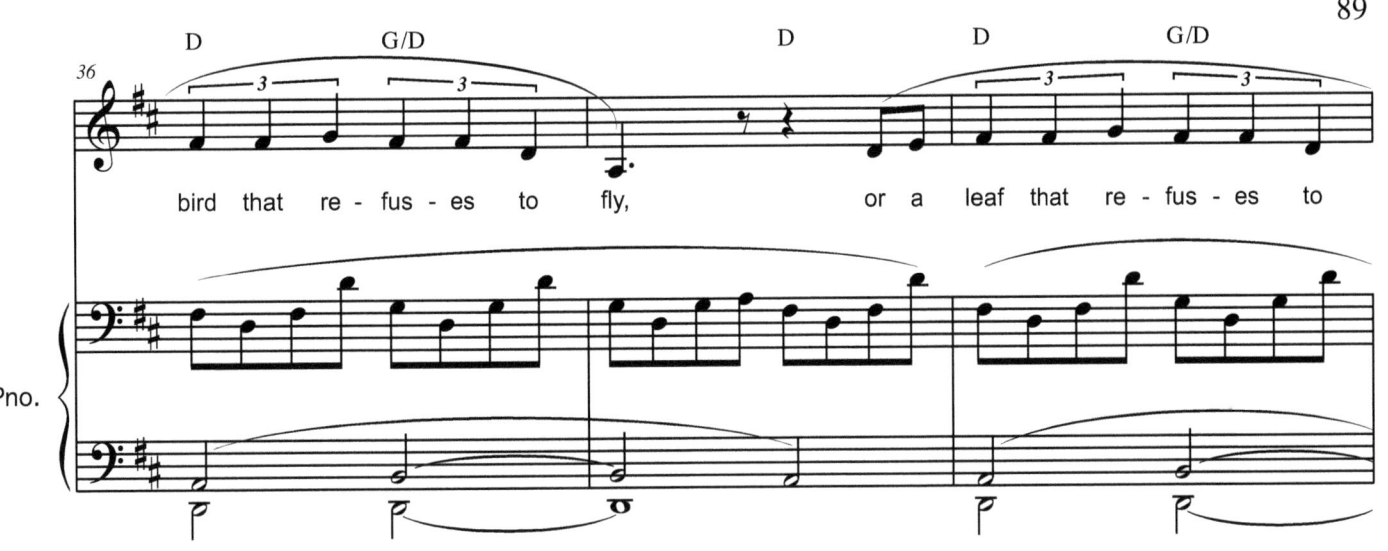
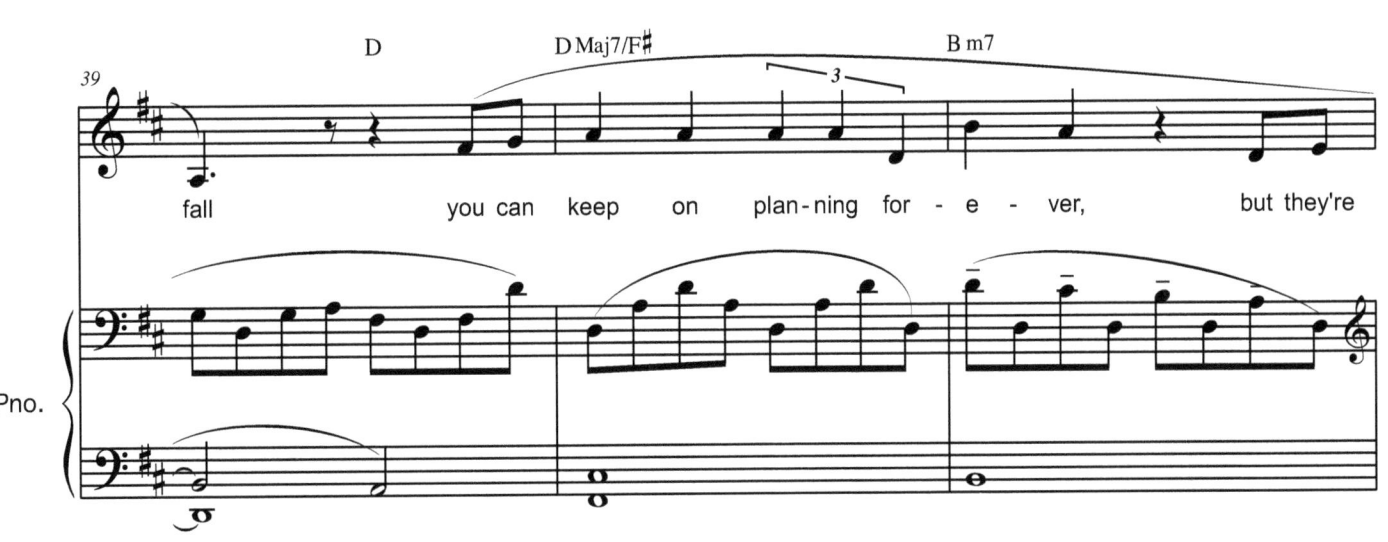
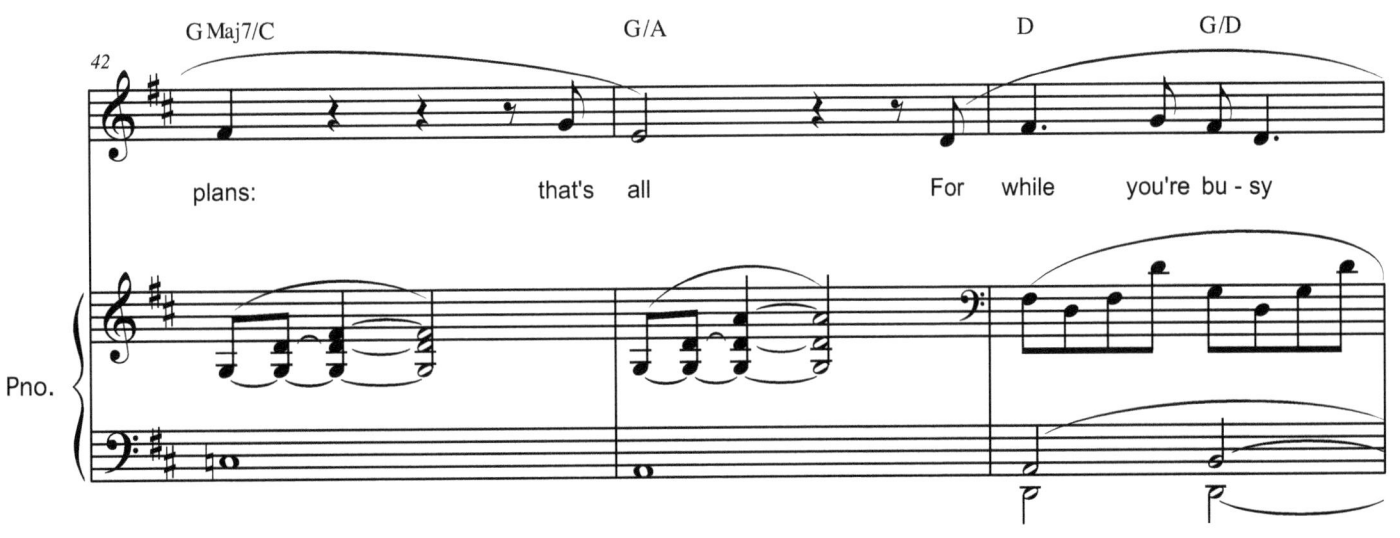

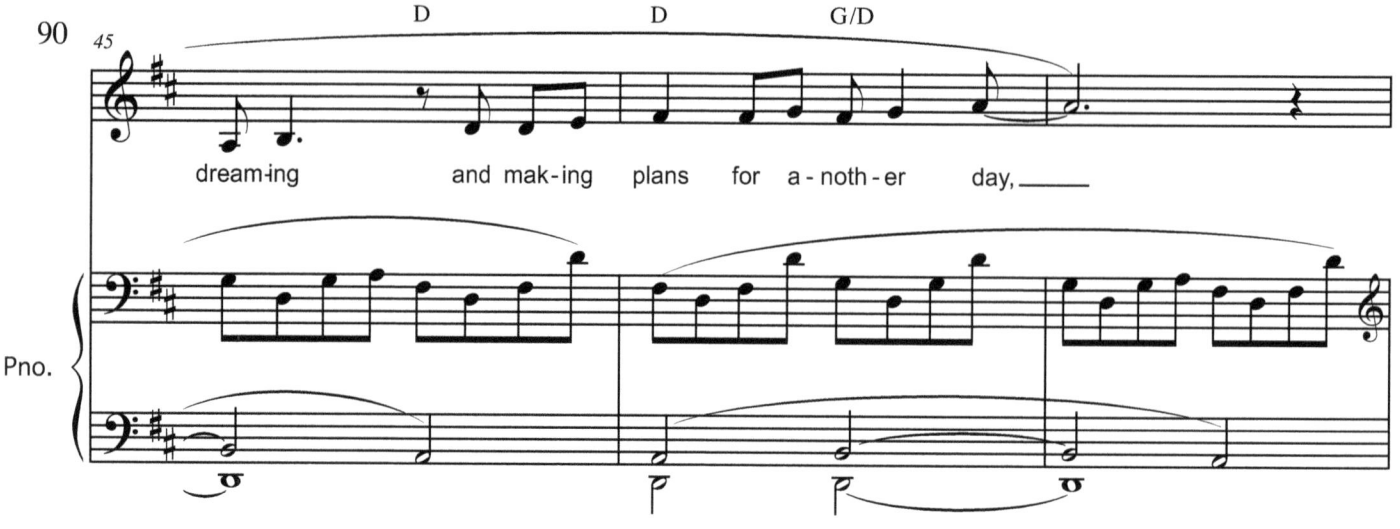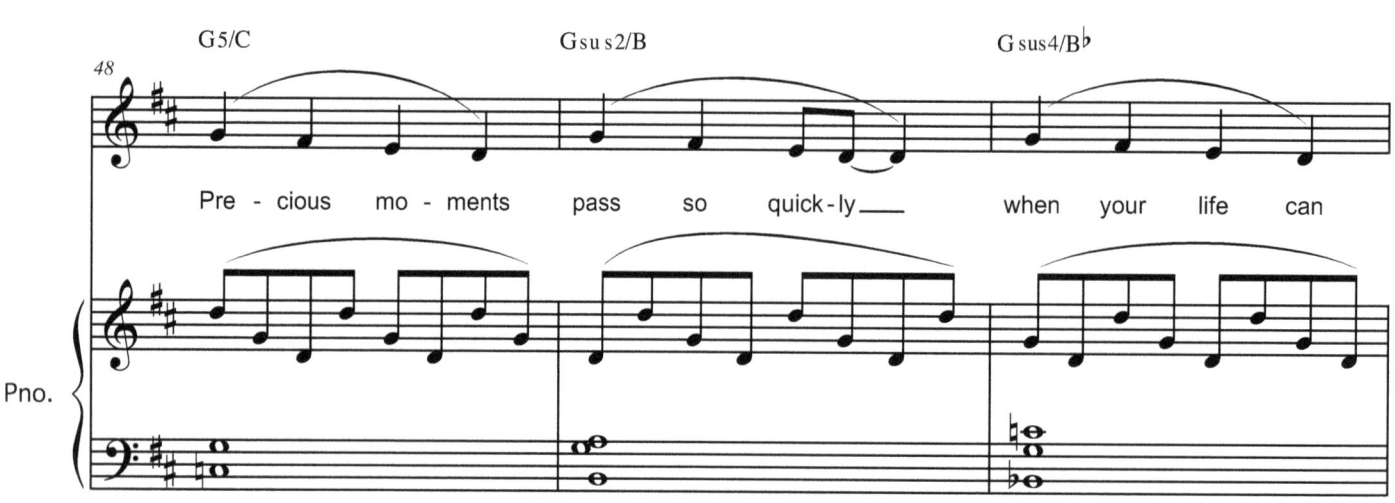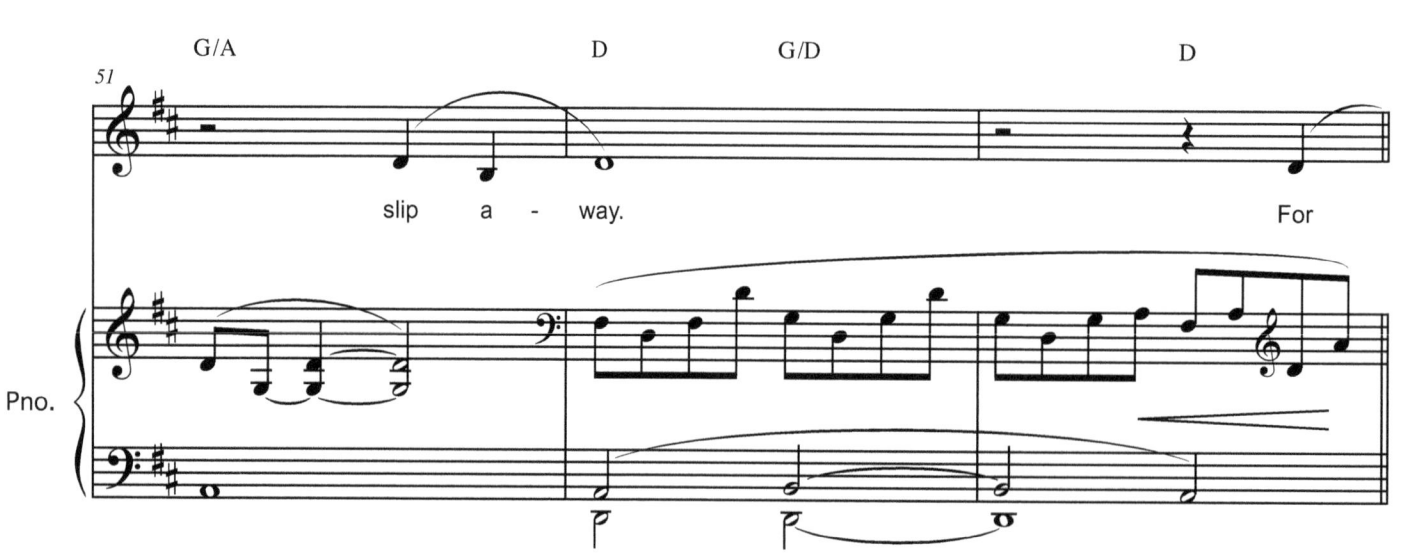

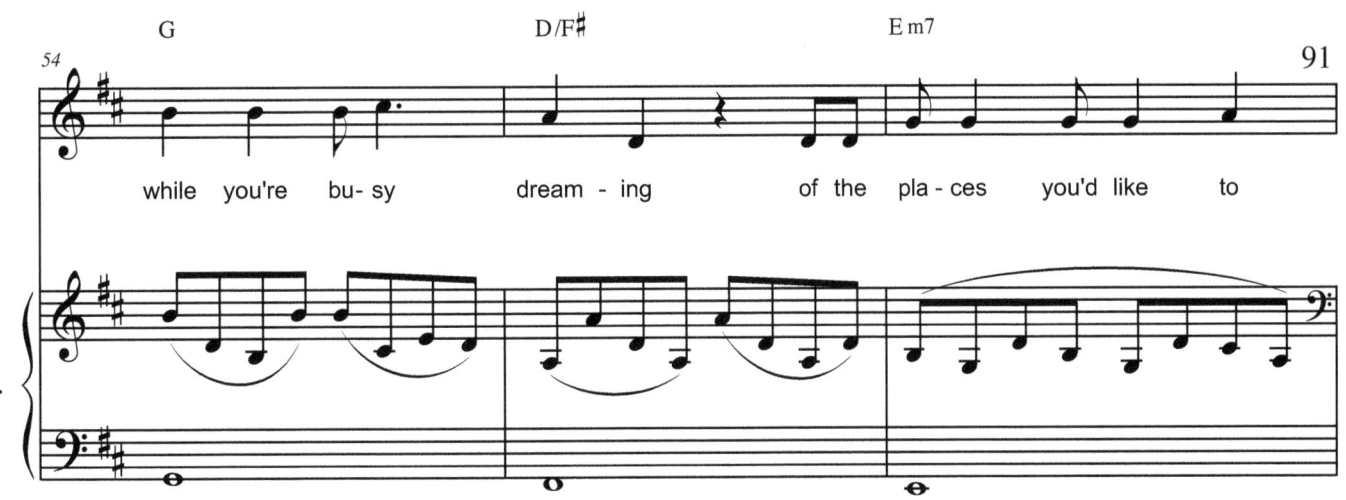
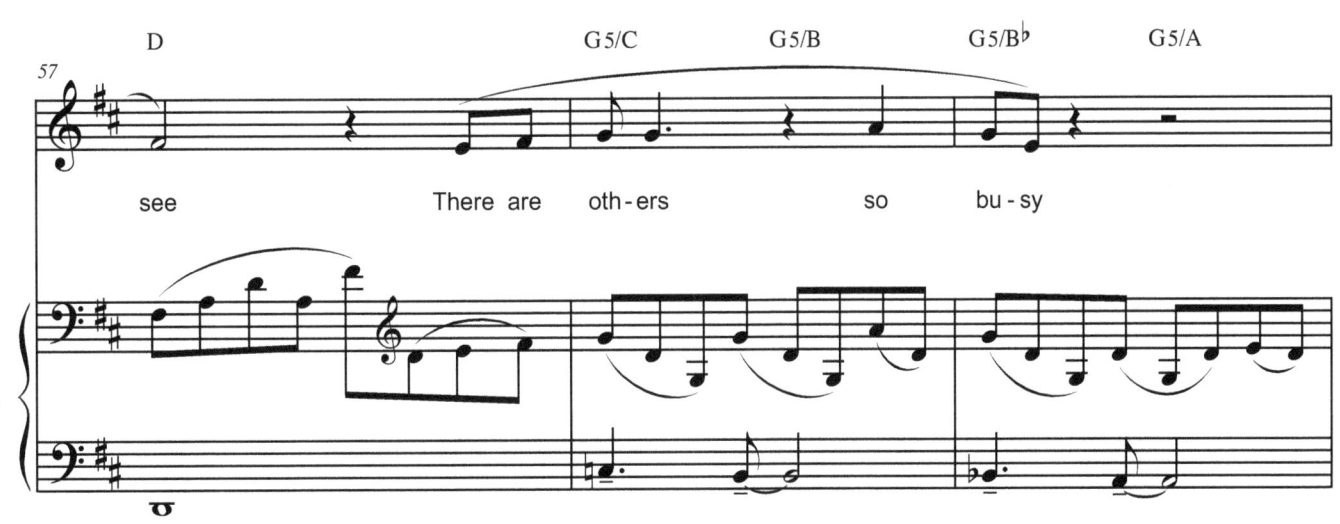

(While You're) Busy Dreaming p 7/8

(While You're) Busy Dreaming p 8/8

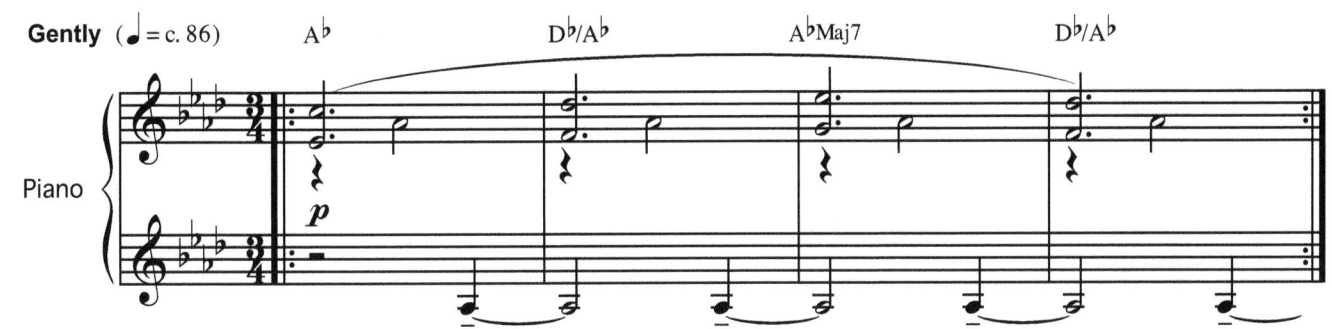

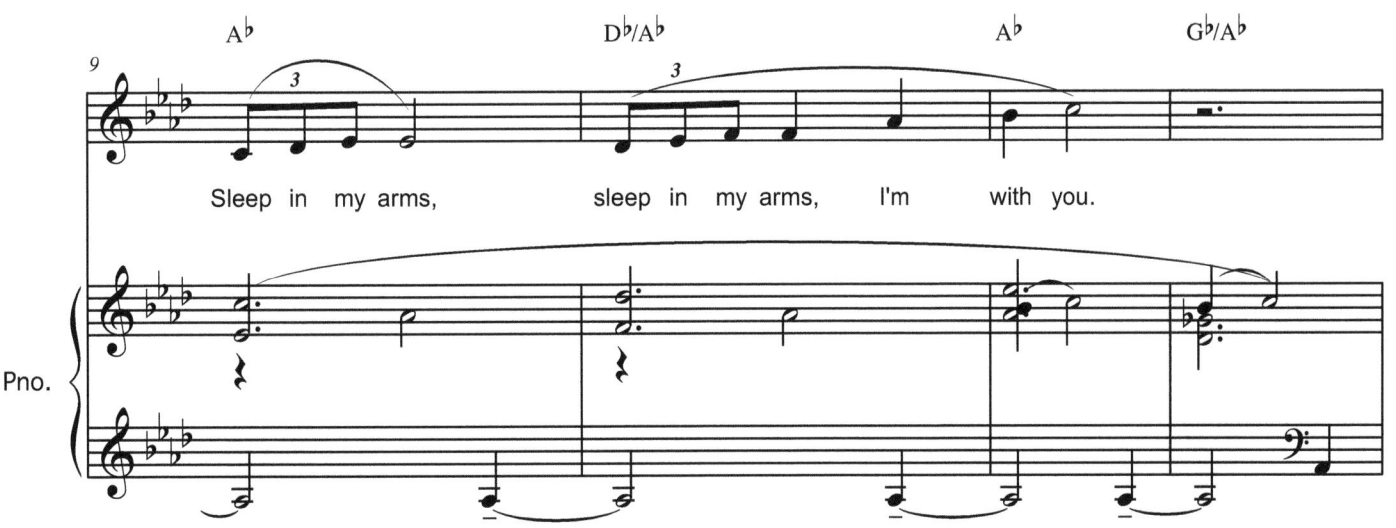

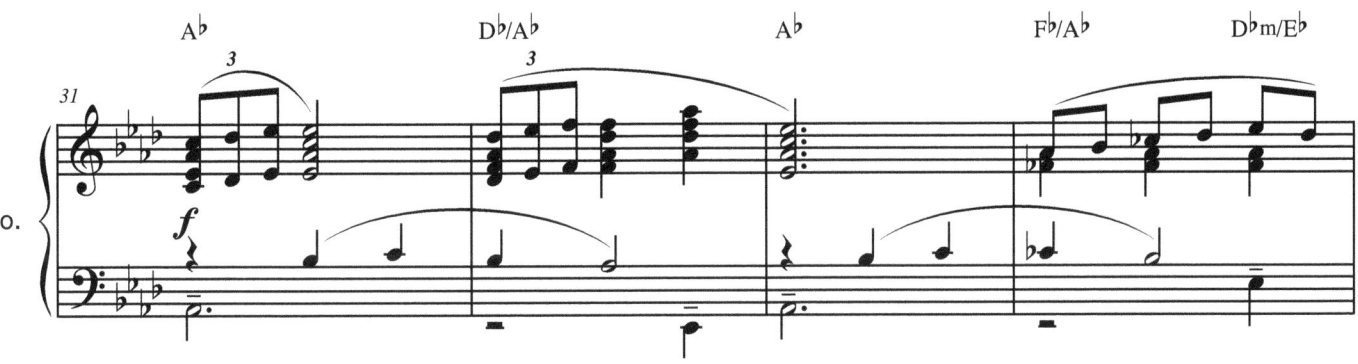
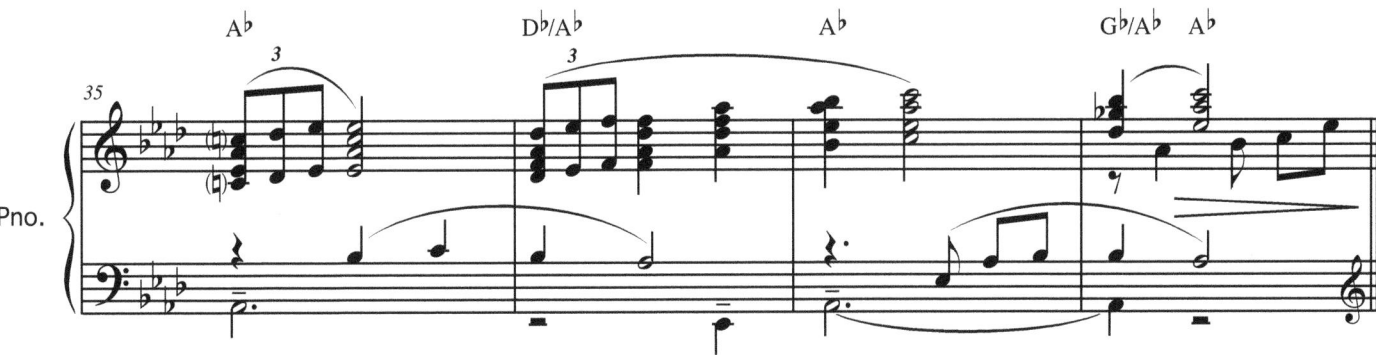

Now you look so peace-ful, qui-et, but in pain.

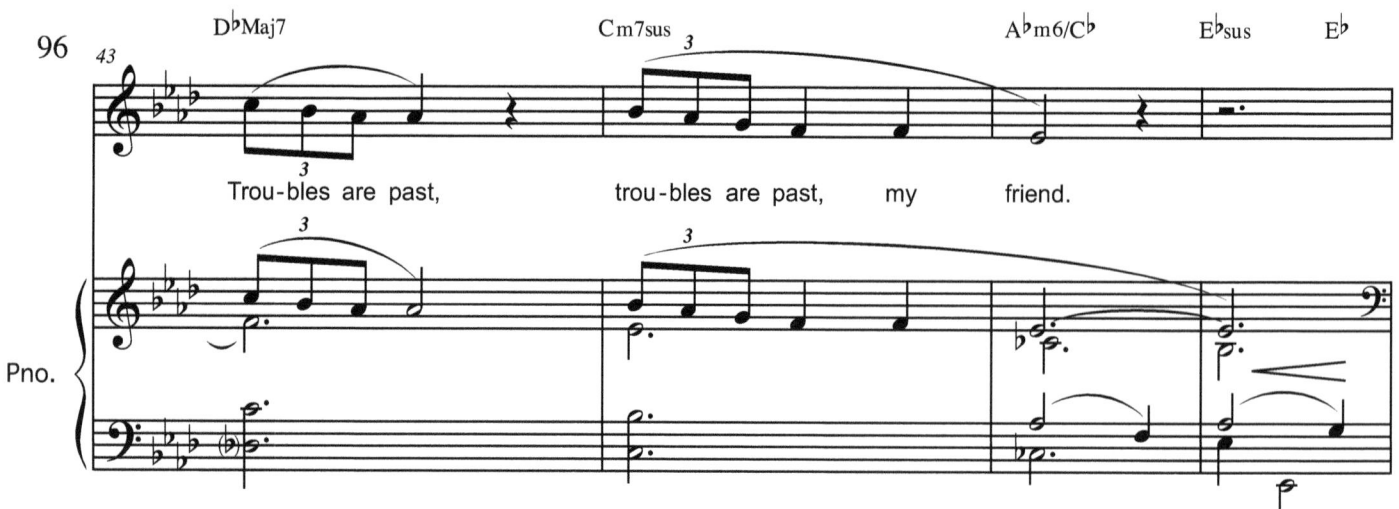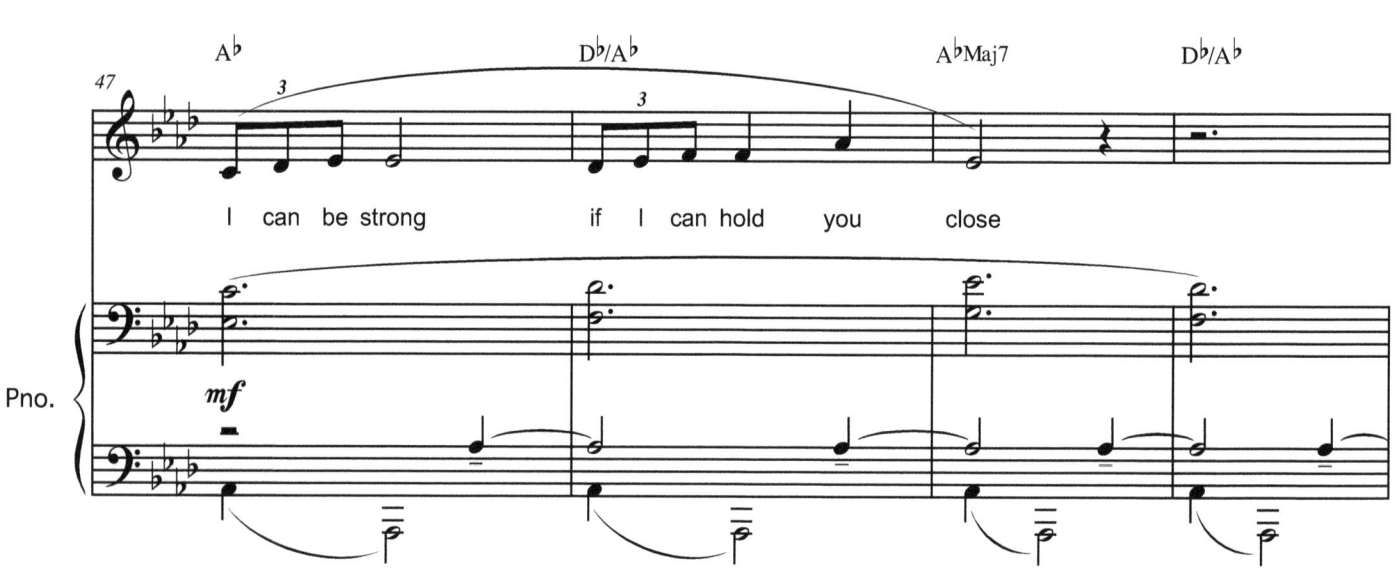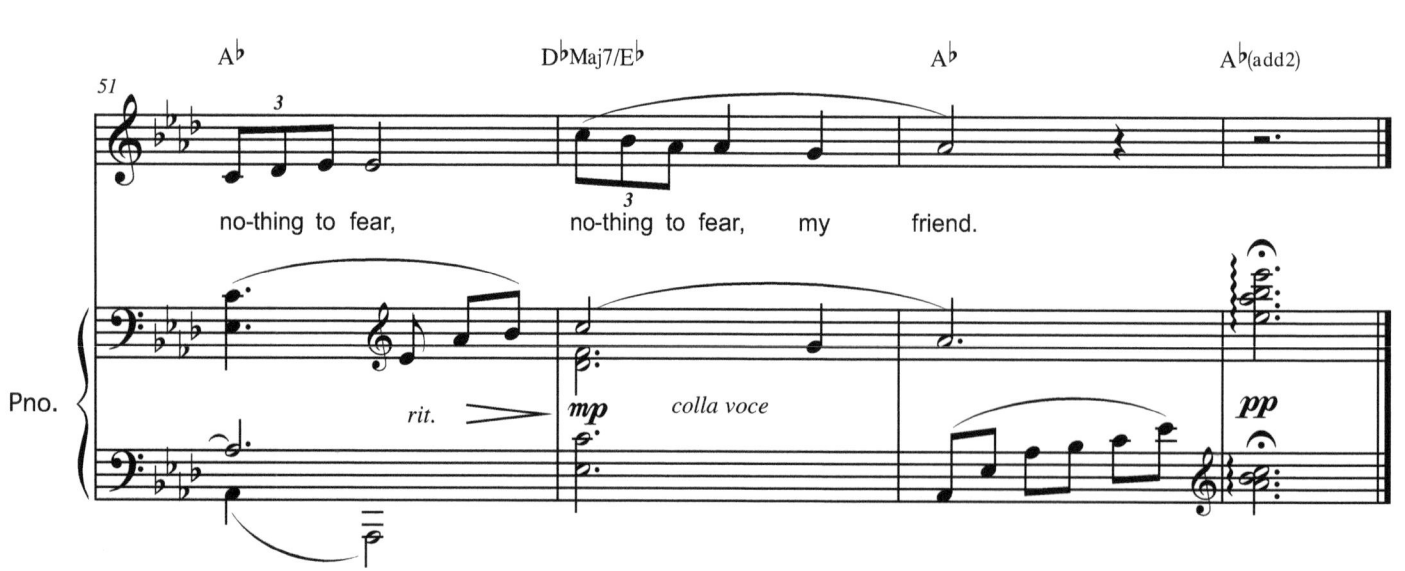

101

103

One Voice p 7/19

104

114

One Voice p 18/19

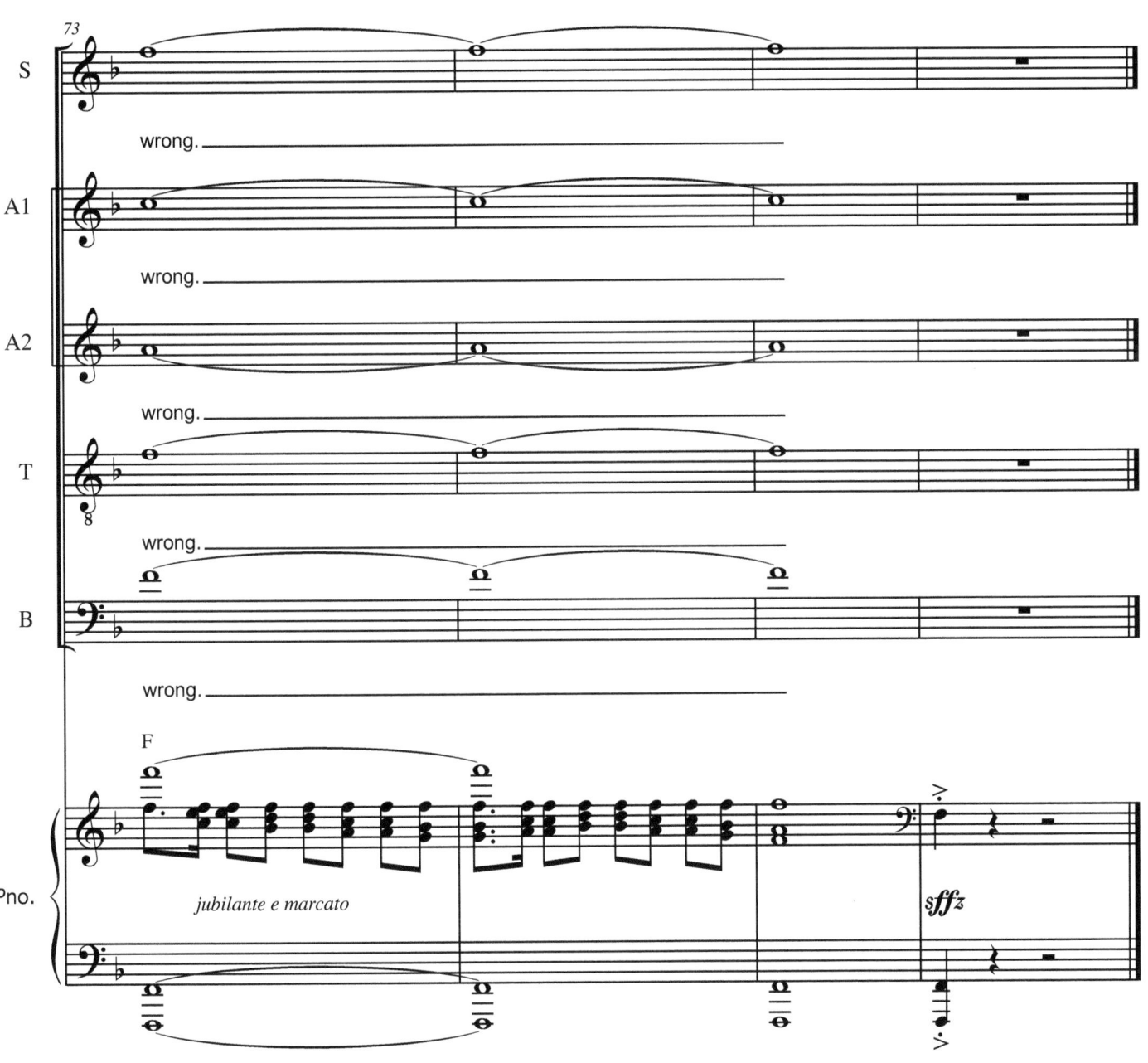

116

Nearly Autumn
The Railway Children

Lyrics by Julian Woolford

Music by Richard John

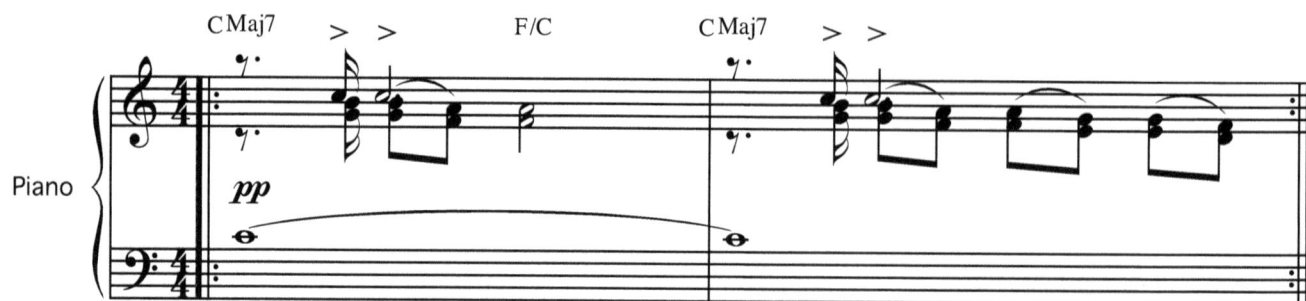

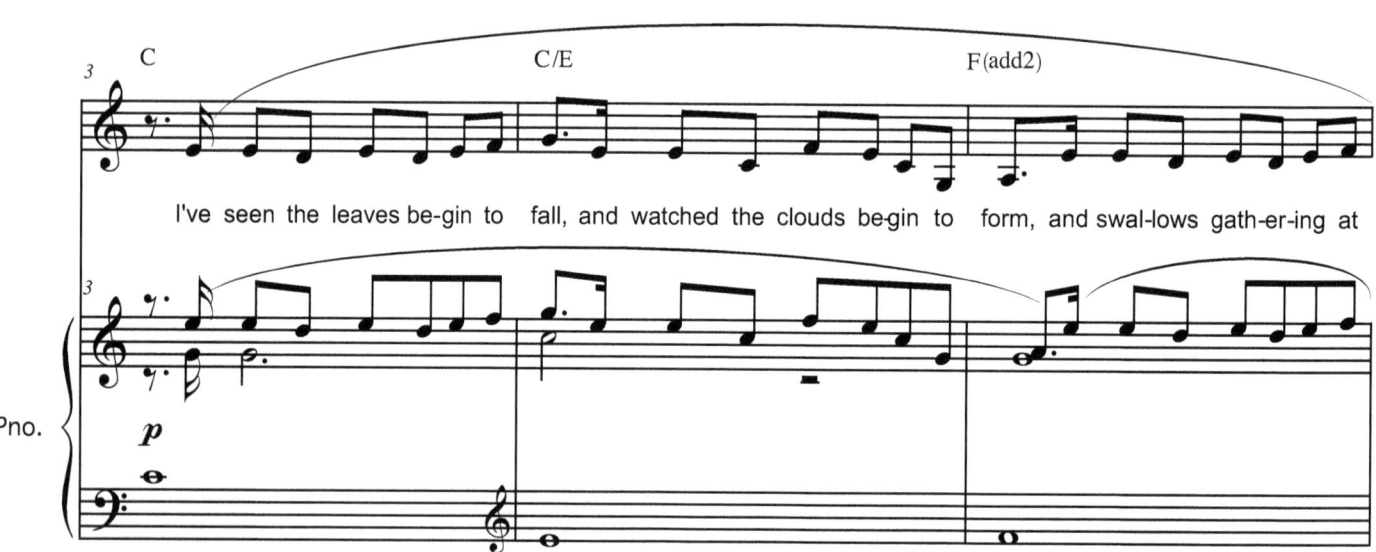

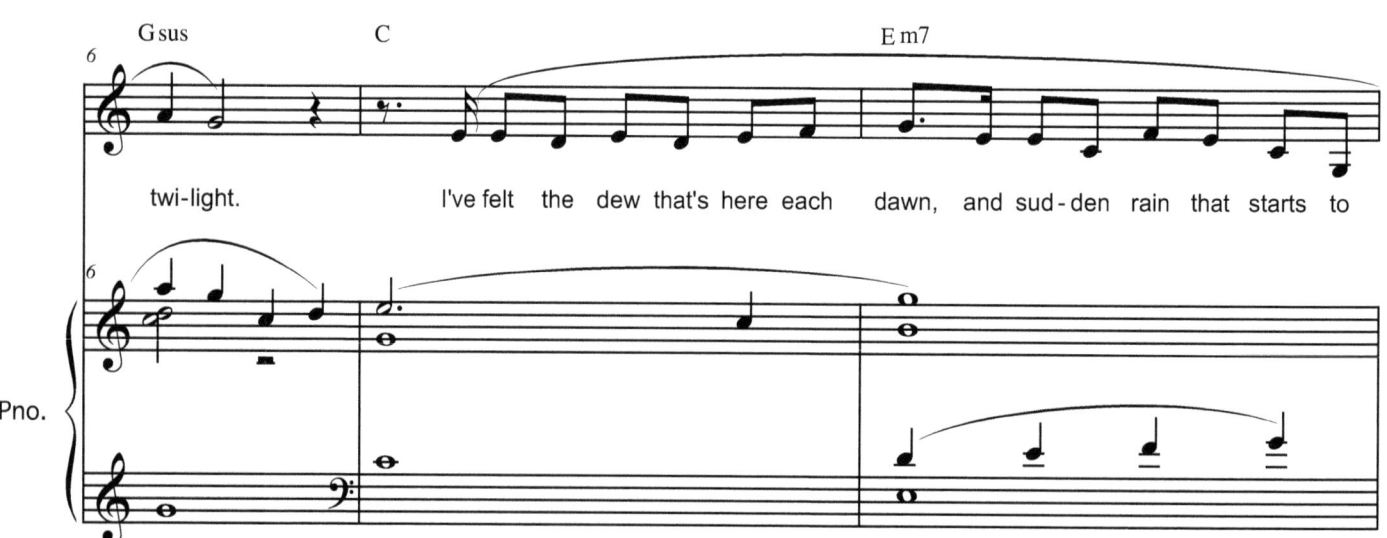

Copyright © Woolford & John 2007
International Copyright Secured. All Rights Reserved.

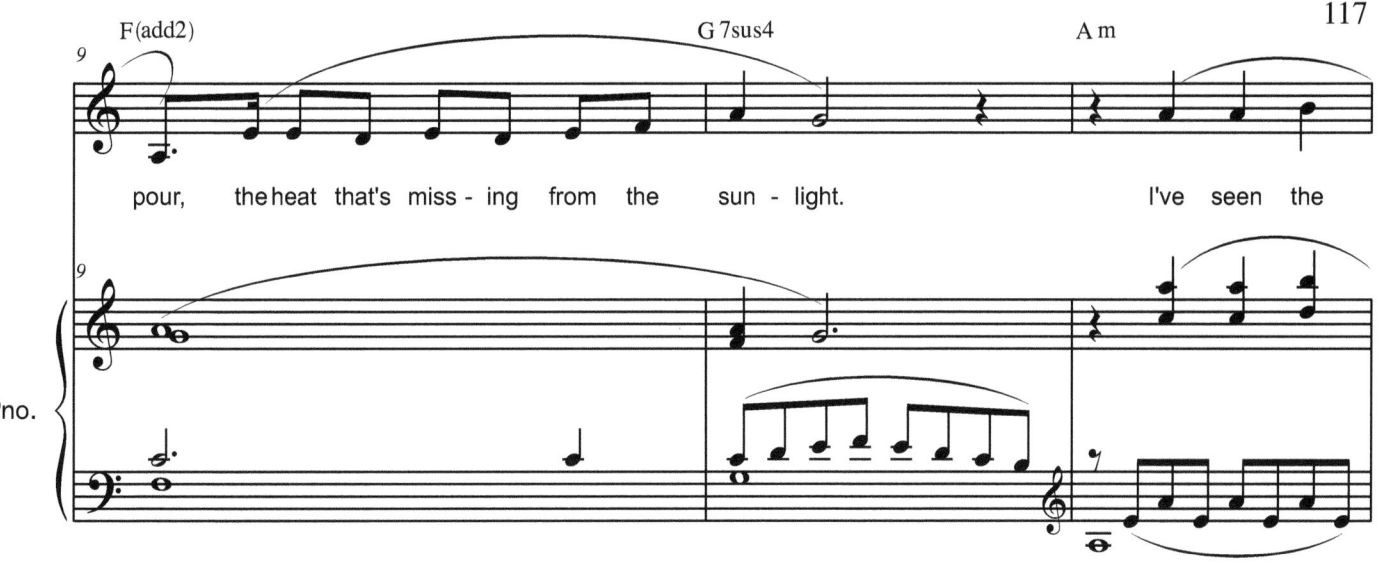
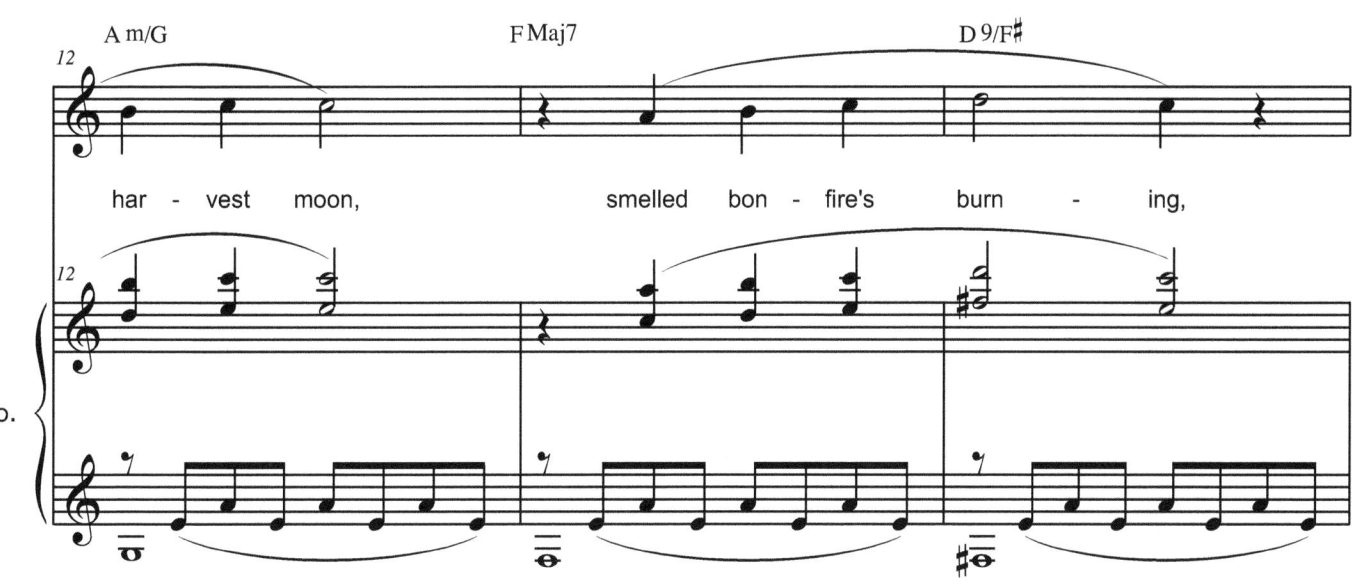
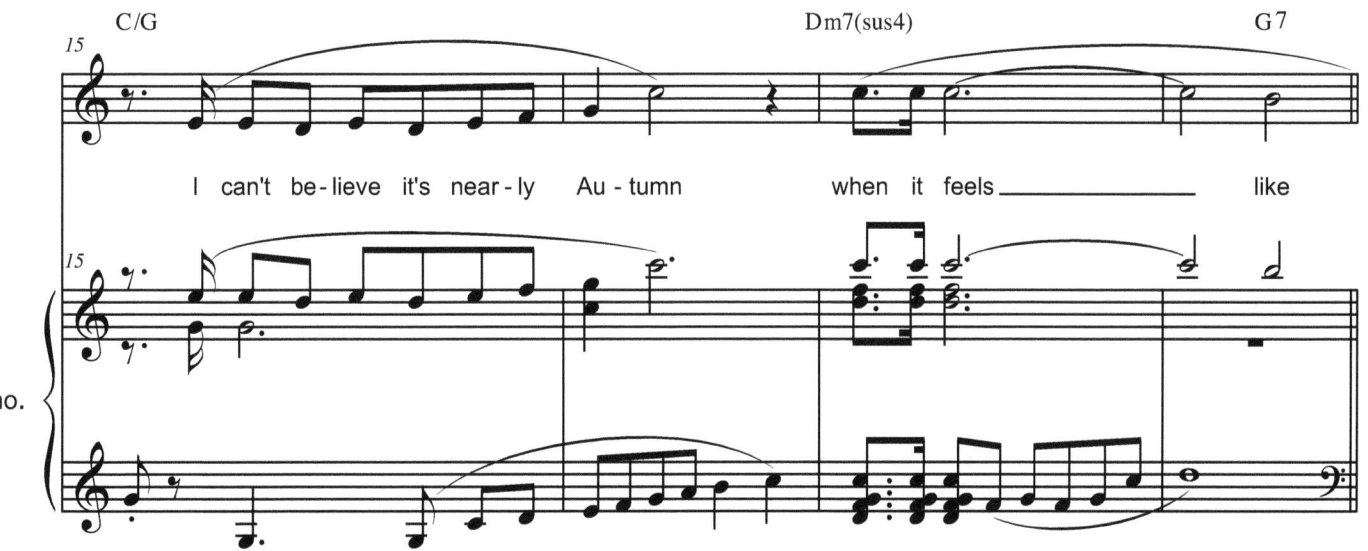

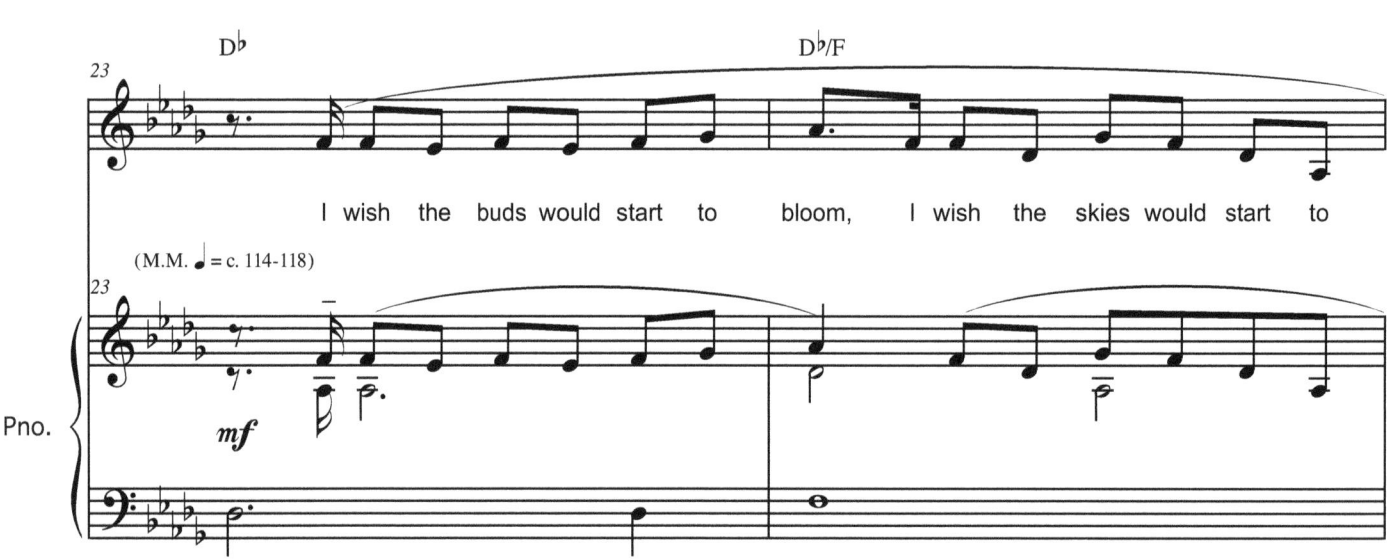
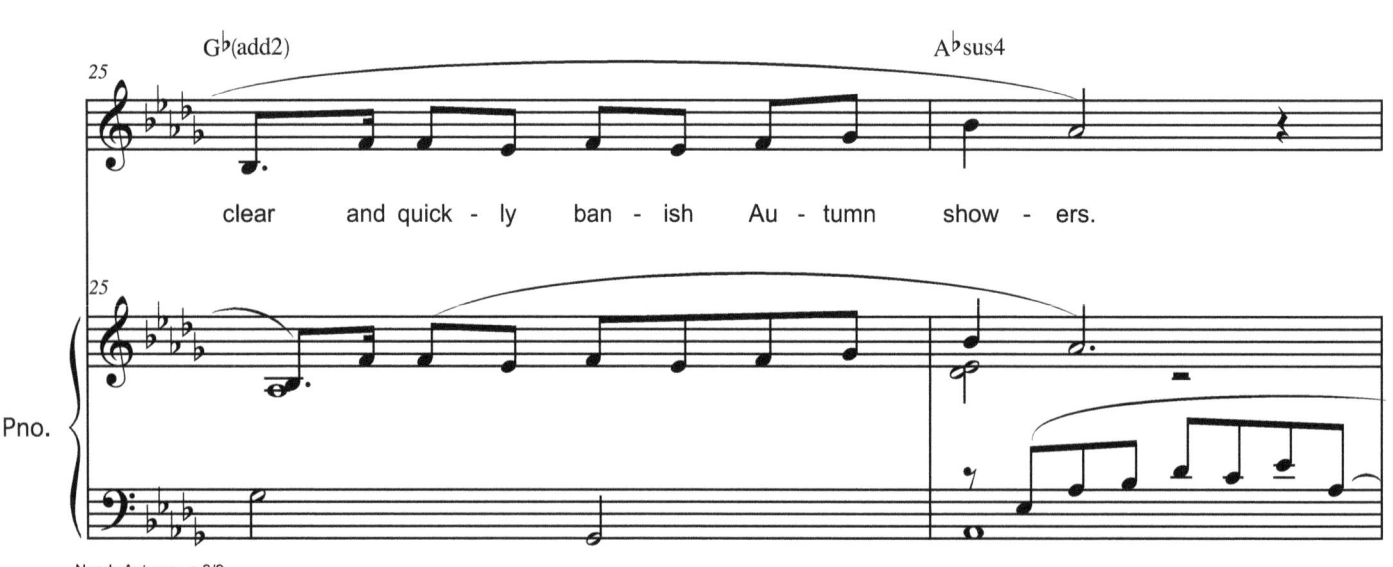

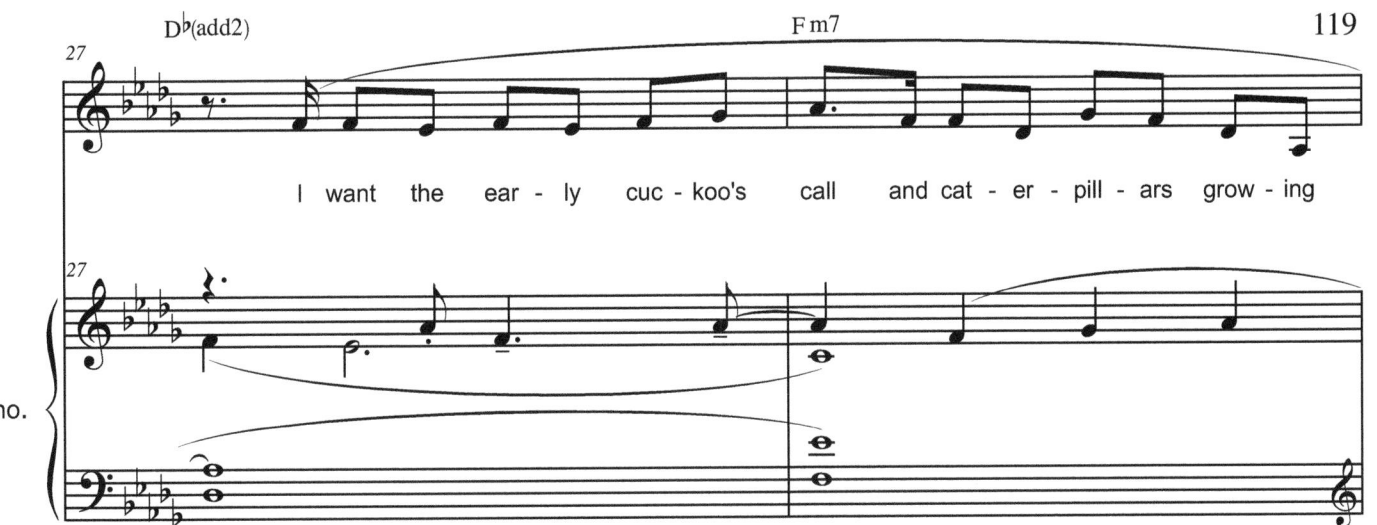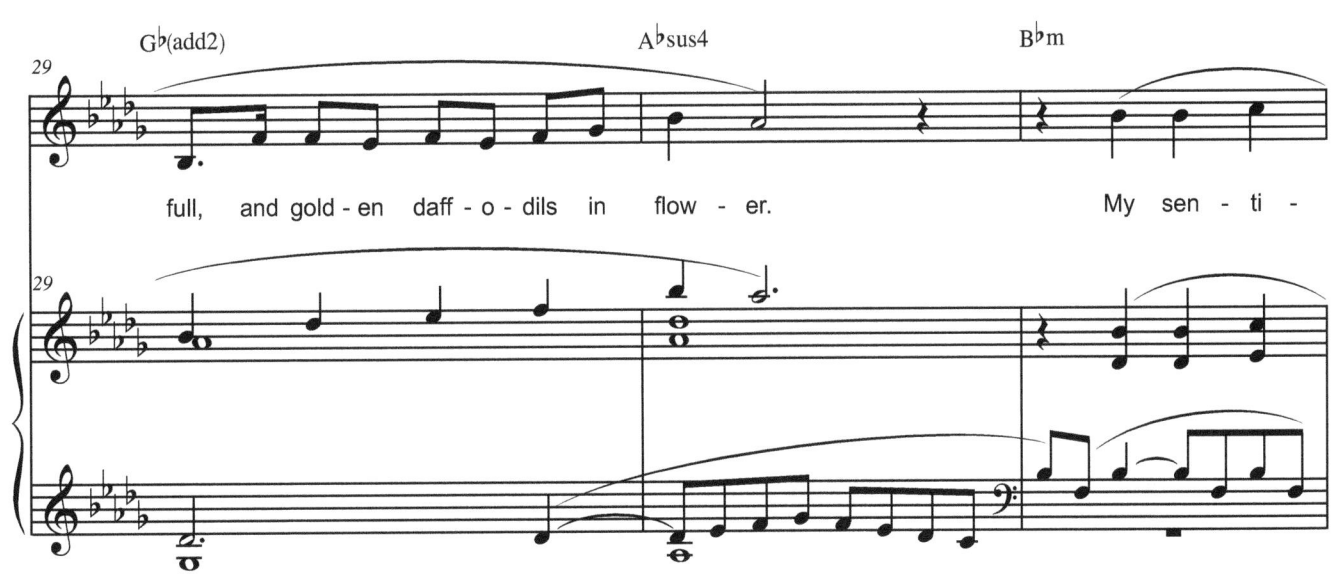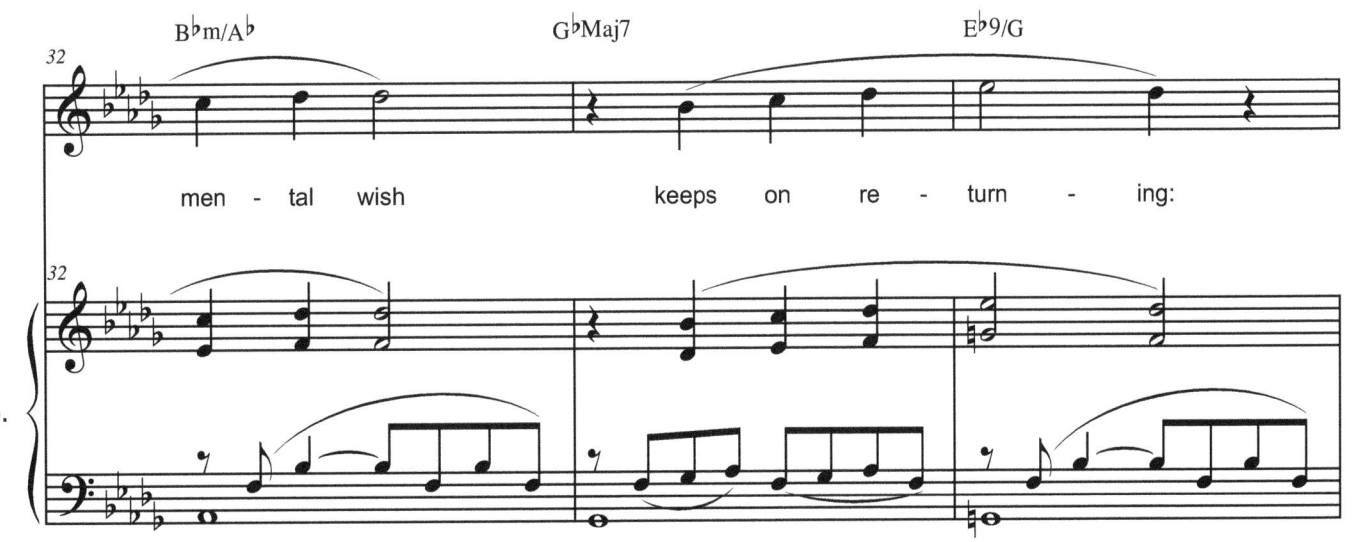

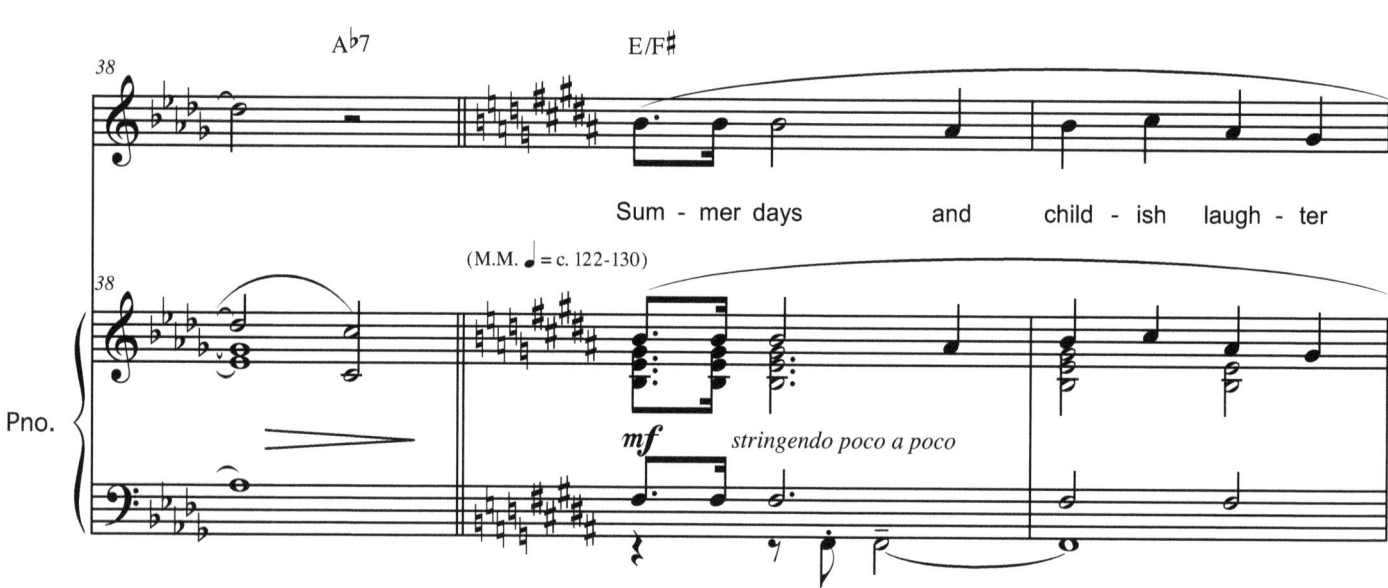
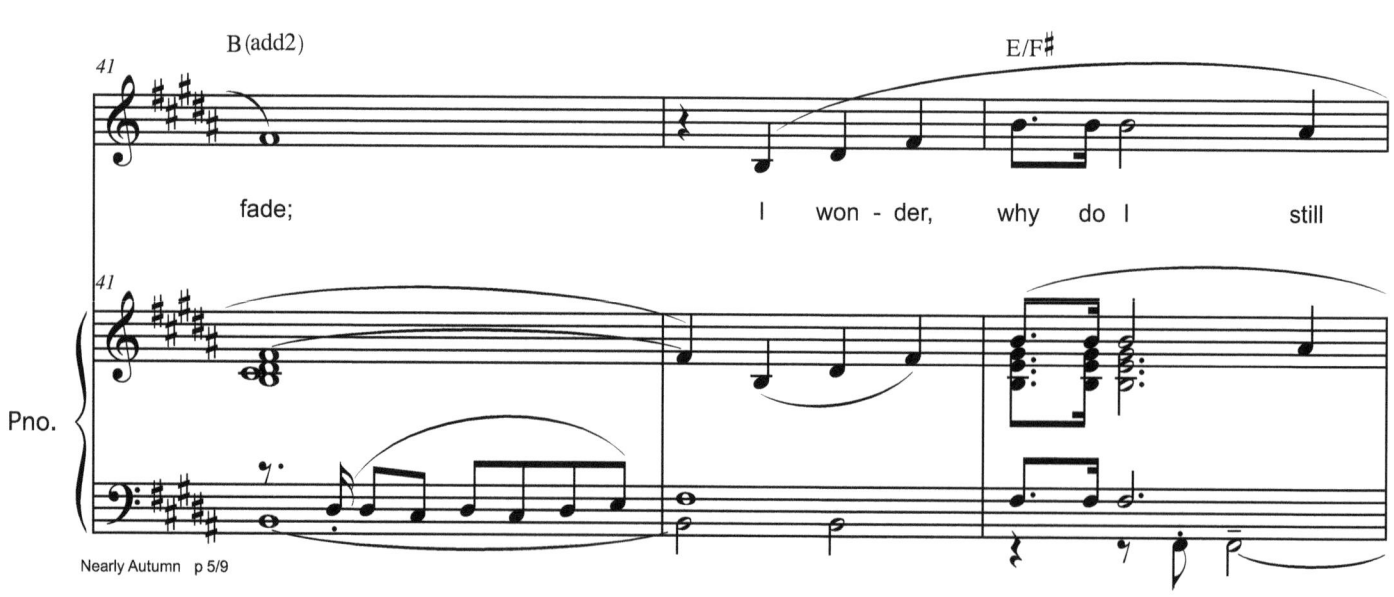

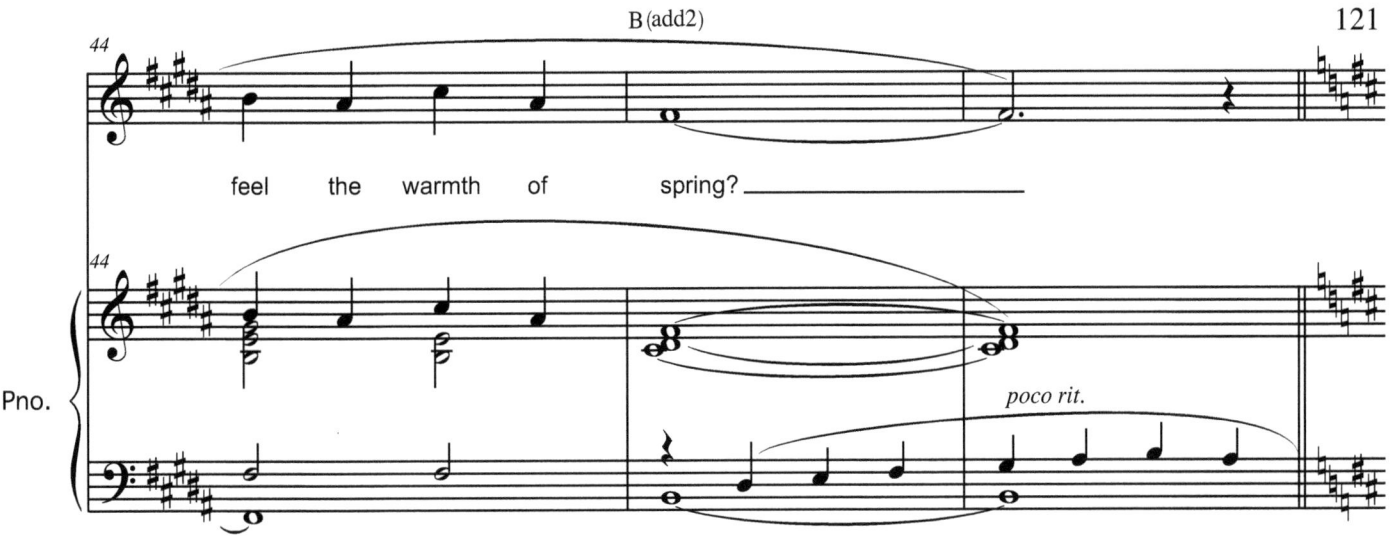
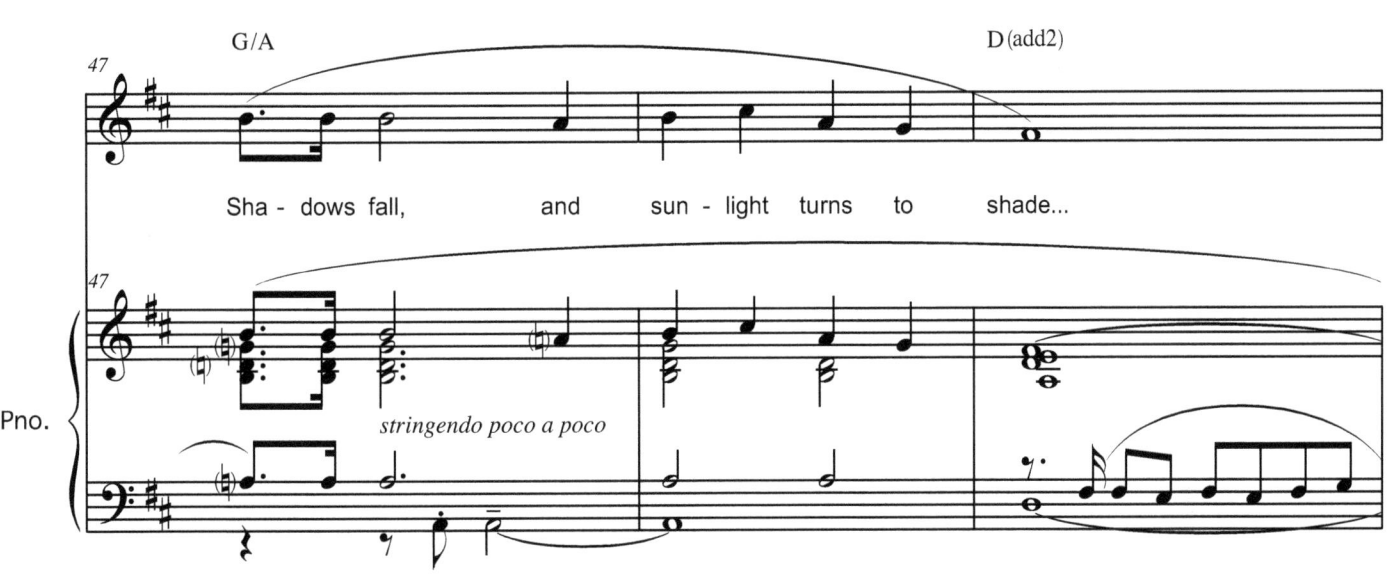
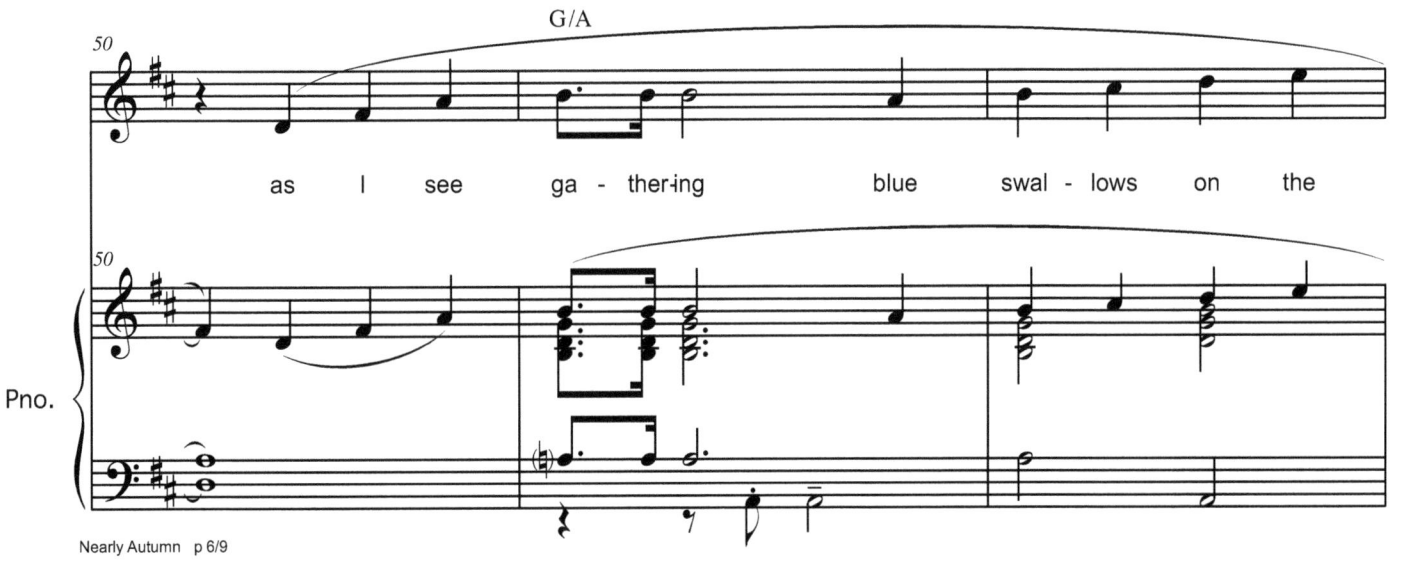

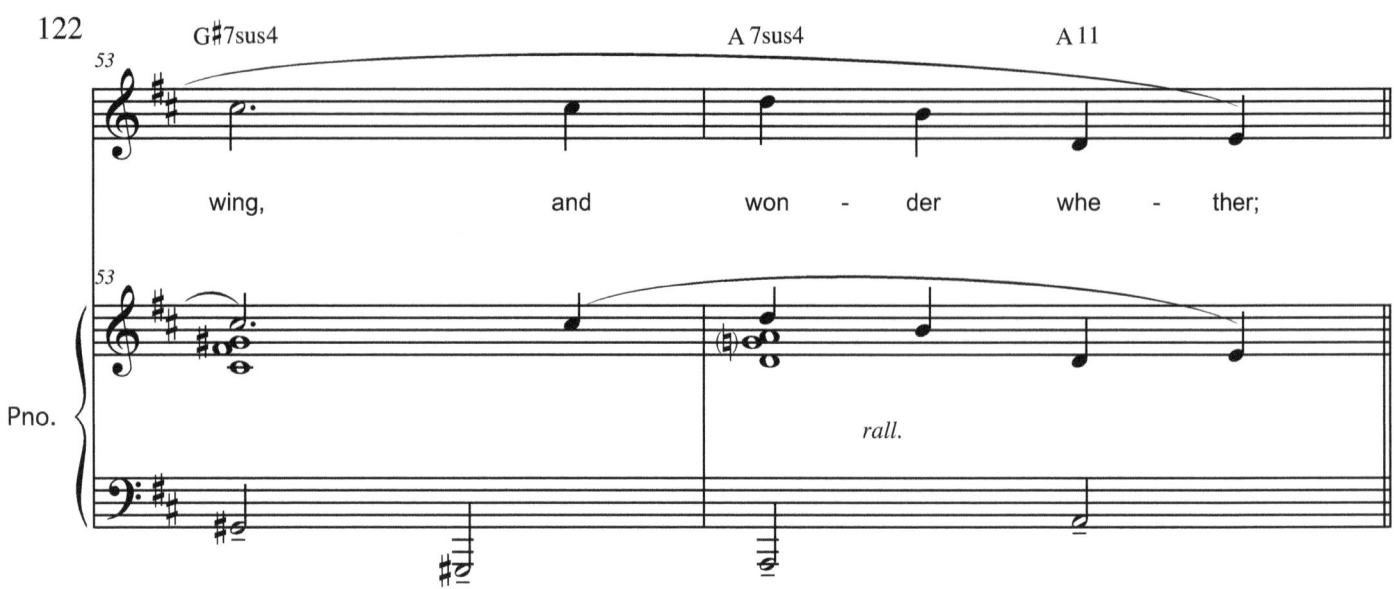
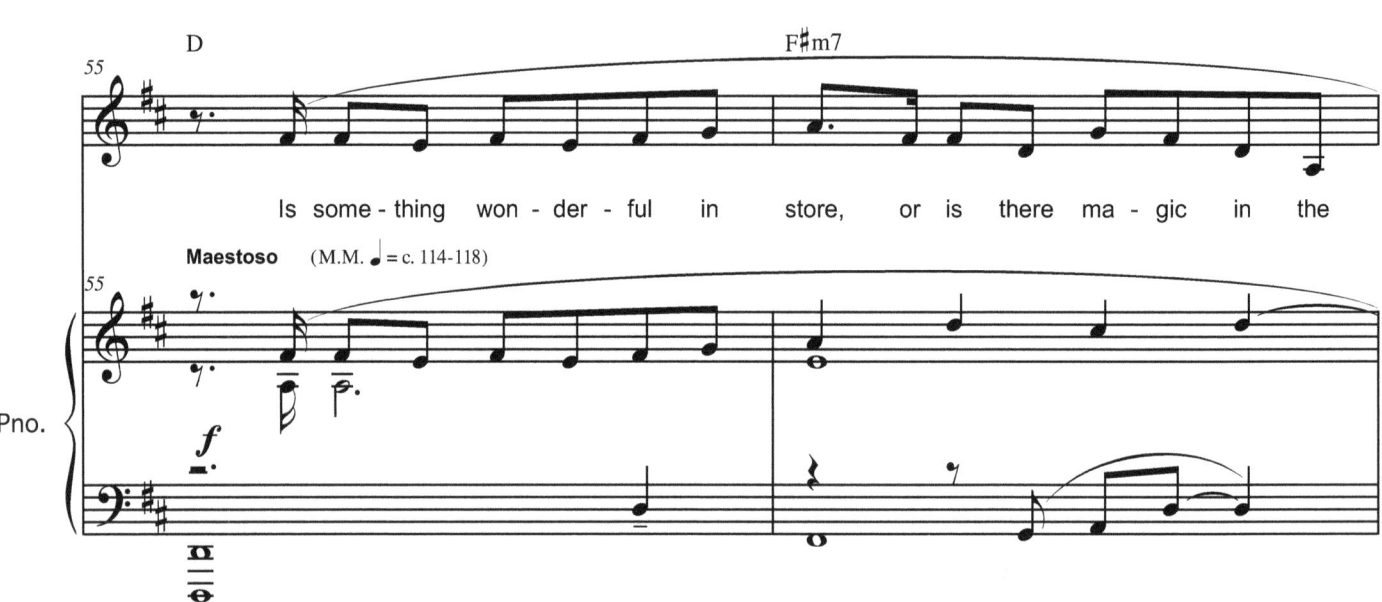
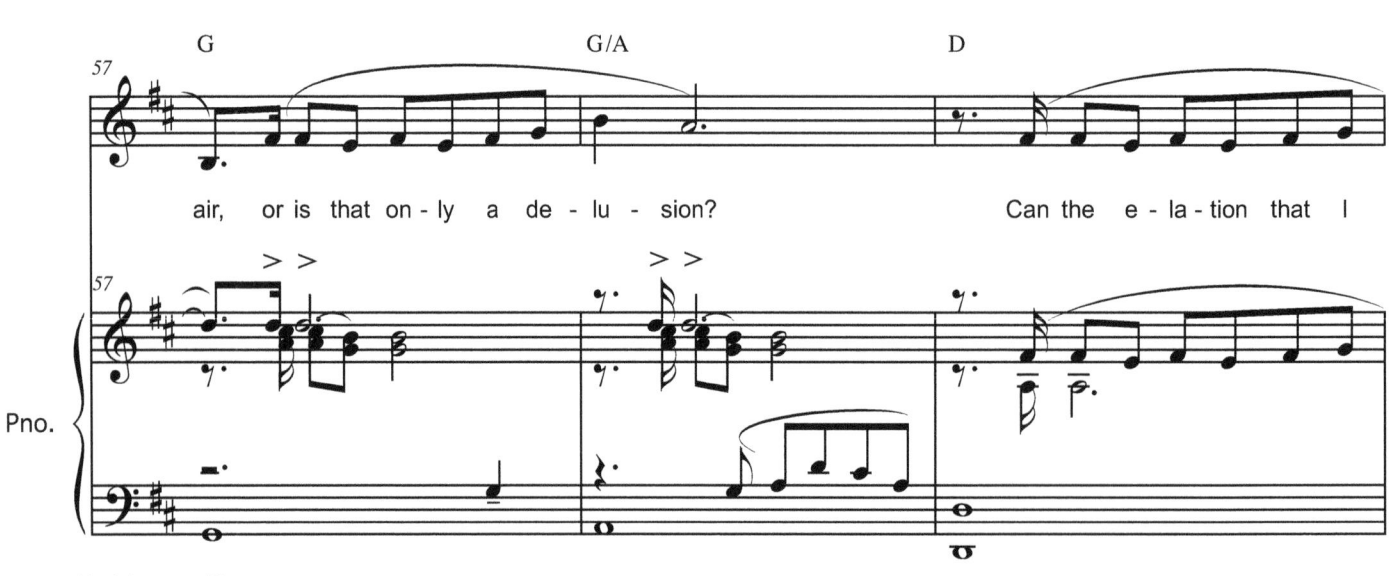

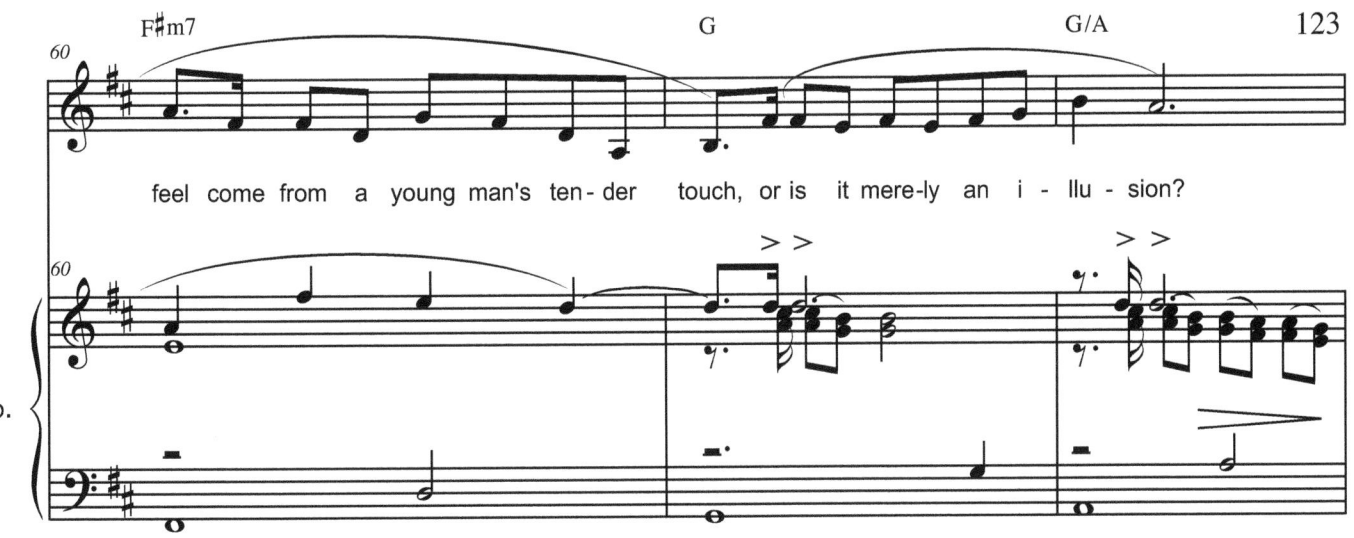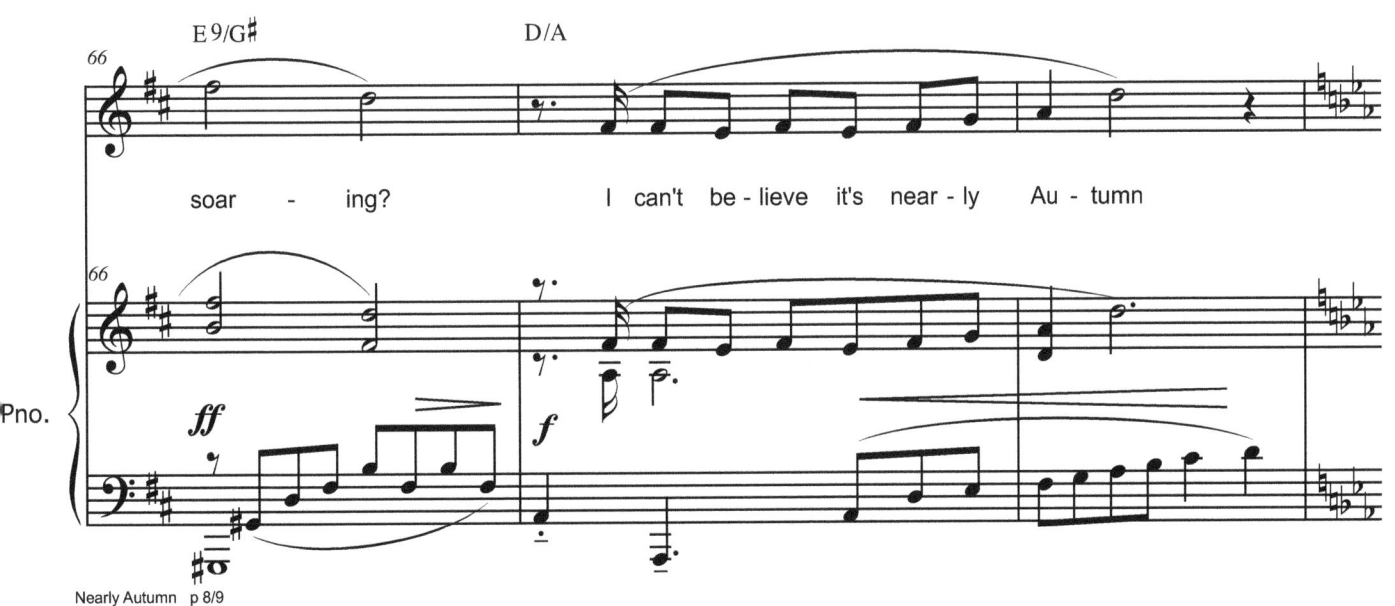

www.ingramcontent.com/pod-product-compliance
Ingram Content Group UK Ltd.
Pitfield, Milton Keynes, MK11 3LW, UK
UKHW050226150426
5217IPUK00023B/1670